HARRAP'S

D0610812

Compiled by
Judith Bryce
Donatella de Ferra
Simona Rizzardi
Gabriella Bacchelli
with
LEXUS

HARRAP

EDINBURGH   PARIS

Distributed in the United States by

PRENTICE HALL
New York

First published in Great Britain 1990
by HARRAP BOOKS Ltd
43–45 Annandale Street, Edinburgh EH7 4AZ

ISBN 0 245-60052-3

Reprinted 1991, 1992, 1993

Printed in England by Clays Ltd, St Ives plc

INTRODUCTION

This Italian grammar has been written to meet the needs of those who are learning Italian and is particularly useful for those taking school examinations. The essential rules of the Italian language have been explained in terms that are as accessible as possible to all users. Where technical terms have been used then full explanations of these terms have also been supplied. There is also a glossary of grammatical terms on pages 9-15. While literary aspects of the language have not been ignored, the emphasis has been placed squarely on modern spoken Italian. This grammar, with its wealth of lively and typical illustrations of usage taken from the present-day language, is the ideal study tool for all levels - from the beginner who is starting to come to grips with the Italian language through to the advanced user who requires a comprehensive and readily accessible work of reference.

Abbreviations used in the text:

fem	feminine
masc	masculine
pl	plural
sing	singular

Note:

Italian examples given in the third person may, theoretically, be translated in various ways since, where no pronoun is given, the third person singular and plural may be equivalent to 'he/she/you' and to 'they/you' respectively. In actual usage, of course, context will decide. In this book we have normally translated third person singular examples with 'he/she' and sometimes with 'you' according to the most probable context of utterance.

CONTENTS

6   CONTENTS

8   CONTENTS

1. GLOSSARY OF GRAMMATICAL TERMS

ABSTRACT NOUN An abstract noun is one which refers not to a concrete physical object or a person but to a quality or a concept. Examples of abstract nouns are *happiness, life, length*.

ACTIVE The active form of a verb is the basic form as in *I remember her*. It is normally opposed to the passive form of the verb as in *she will be remembered*.

ADJECTIVAL NOUN An adjectival noun is an adjective used as a noun. For example, the adjective *young* is used as a noun in *the young at heart*.

ADJECTIVE A describing word telling us what something or someone is like (eg *a small house, the Royal family, an interesting pastime*).

ADVERB Adverbs are normally used with a verb to add extra information by indicating how the action is done (adverbs of manner), **when, where** and with **how much intensity** the action is done (adverbs of time, place and intensity), or **to what extent** the action is done (adverbs of quantity). Adverbs may also be used with an adjective or another adverb (eg *a very attractive girl, very well*).

AGREEMENT In Italian, words such as adjectives, articles and pronouns are said to agree in number and gender with the word they refer to. This means that their ending (or form) changes according to the **number** of the noun (singular or plural) and its **gender** (masculine or feminine).

ANTECEDENT The antecedent of a relative pronoun is the word or words to which the relative pronoun refers.

The antecedent is usually found directly before the relative pronoun (eg in the sentence *I know **the man** who did this*, ***the man*** is the antecedent of *who*).

APPOSITION
A word or a phrase is said to be in apposition to another when it is placed directly after it without any joining word (eg *Mr Jones, **our bank manager**, rang today*).

ARTICLE
See DEFINITE ARTICLE, INDEFINITE ARTICLE and PARTITIVE ARTICLE.

AUGMENTATIVE
An augmentative is added to a noun to indicate largeness, eg *ragazzo (boy)*, ***ragazzone** (big boy)*.

AUXILIARY
Auxiliary verbs are used to form compound tenses of other verbs, eg ***have** in I **have** seen* or ***will** in she **will** go*. The main auxiliary verbs in Italian are *avere* (to have) and *essere* (to be). See MODAL AUXILIARIES.

CARDINAL
Cardinal numbers are numbers such as *one, two, ten, fourteen*, as opposed to **ordinal** numbers (eg *first, second*).

CLAUSE
A clause is a group of words which contains at least a subject and a verb: *he said* is a clause. A clause often contains more than this basic information, eg *he said this to her yesterday*. Sentences can be made up of several clauses, eg *he said/he'd call me/if he were free*. See SENTENCE.

COMPARATIVE
The comparative forms of adjectives and adverbs allow us to compare two things, persons or actions. In English, *more ... than, ...er than, less ... than* and *as ... as* are used for comparison.

COMPOUND TENSES
Compound tenses are tenses consisting of more than one element. In Italian, the compound tenses of a verb are formed by the **auxiliary** verb and the **past participle**: *ho visto, è venuto*.

COMPOUND NOUNS
Compound nouns are nouns made up of two or more separate words. English examples are *goalkeeper* or *dinner party*.

CONDITIONAL
This mood is used to describe what someone would do, or something that would happen if a condition was fulfilled (eg *I **would come** if I was well; the chair **would have broken** if he had sat on it*). It also indicates the future in the past, eg *he said he **would come***.

CONJUGATION

The conjugation of a verb is the set of different forms taken in the particular tenses of that verb.

CONJUNCTION

Conjunctions are linking words. They may be coordinating or subordinating. Coordinating conjunctions are words like *and, but, or*; subordinating conjunctions are words like *because, after, although*.

COUNTABLE

A noun is countable if it can form a plural and if it can be used with the indefinite article. Examples of countable nouns are *house, car, sweater*.

DEFINITE ARTICLE

The definite article is *the* in English and *il, lo, la, l', i, gli* and *le* in Italian.

DEMONSTRATIVE

Demonstrative adjectives (eg *this, that, these*) and pronouns (eg *this one, that one*) are used to point out a particular person or object.

DIMINUTIVE

A diminutive is added to a noun (or to an adjective) to indicate smallness or a favourable attitude by the speaker, eg *ragazzo (boy)*, **ragazzino** *(small boy)*.

DIRECT OBJECT

A noun or a pronoun which in English follows a verb without any linking preposition, eg *I met a friend*. Note that in English a preposition is often omitted, eg *I sent him a present - him* is equivalent to *to him - a present* is the direct object.

ELISION

Elision is when the last letter of certain words (*lo, la, una, di*) is replaced with an apostrophe (') before a word starting with a **vowel** or a **silent h** (eg *l'uomo, un'amica, d'arancia, d'hotel*).

ENDING

The ending of a verb is determined by the **person** (1st/2nd/3rd) and **number** (singular/plural) of its subject. In Italian, most tenses have six different endings. The ending of a noun can often indicate whether it is masculine or feminine and singular or plural. See PERSON and NUMBER.

EXCLAMATION

Words or sentences used to express surprise, annoyance etc (eg *what!, wow!, how lucky!, what a nice day!*).

FEMININE

See GENDER.

GENDER

The gender of a noun indicates whether the noun is **masculine** or **feminine**. In Italian, the gender of a noun is not always determined by the sex of what it refers to.

GERUND	A gerund (also called a 'verbal noun' in English) is like the word *skiing* in *skiing is fun* and *waiting* in *I'm fed up with waiting*. In Italian, gerunds cannot be nouns.
IDIOMATIC	Idiomatic expressions (or idioms), are expressions which cannot normally be translated word for word. For example, *it's raining cats and dogs* is translated by *piove a catinelle* (literally: *it's raining by the basinful*).
IMPERATIVE	A mood used for giving orders (eg *stop!, don't go!*) or for making suggestions (eg *let's go*).
INDEFINITE	Indefinite pronouns and adjectives are words that do not refer to a definite person or object (eg *each, someone, every*).
INDEFINITE ARTICLE	The indefinite article is *a, an* in English and *un, uno, una, un'* in Italian.
INDICATIVE	The form of a verb normally used in making statements or asking questions (eg *I like, he came, we are trying, do you see?*). It is opposed to the subjunctive, conditional and imperative.
INDIRECT OBJECT	A pronoun or noun which follows a verb sometimes with a linking preposition (usually *to*), eg *I spoke to my friend/him, she gave him a kiss*.
INFINITIVE	The infinitive is the form of the verb as found in dictionaries. Thus *to eat, to finish, to take* are infinitives. In Italian, the infinitive is recognized by its ending: *-are, -ere* or *-ire* (eg *amare, vedere, finire*).
INTERROGATIVE	Interrogative words are used to ask a **question**. This may be a direct question (*when will you arrive?*) or an indirect question (*I don't know when he'll arrive*). See QUESTION.
MASCULINE	See GENDER.
MODAL AUXILIARIES	In Italian, the modal auxiliaries are *dovere (to have to), potere (to be able to)* and *volere (to want to)*.
MOOD	The name given to the four main areas within which a verb is conjugated. See INDICATIVE, SUBJUNCTIVE, CONDITIONAL, IMPERATIVE.

NOUN	A word which can refer to living creatures, things, places or abstract ideas, eg *postman*, *cat*, *shop*, *passport*, *life*.
NUMBER	The number of a noun indicates whether the noun is **singular** or **plural**. A singular noun refers to one single thing or person (eg *boy*, *train*) and a plural noun to several (eg *boys*, *trains*).
OBJECT	See DIRECT OBJECT, INDIRECT OBJECT.
ORDINAL	Ordinal numbers are *first*, *second*, *third*, *fourth* etc.
PARTITIVE ARTICLE	The partitive articles are *some* and *any* in English and *del*, *dello*, *della*, *dell'*, *dei*, *degli* and *delle*, (as in *del pane*, *delle banane* etc) in Italian.
PASSATO PROSSIMO	This term has been used in the conjugation tables for the compound past tense known in English as the **perfect tense** (eg *I have eaten*).
PASSATO REMOTO	This term has been used in the conjugation tables for the simple past tense known in English as the **past definite** or **past historic** (eg *I ate*).
PASSIVE	A verb is used in the passive when the subject of the verb does not perform the action but is subjected to it. The passive is often formed with a part of the verb **to be** and the past participle of the verb, eg *he was rewarded*.
PAST PARTICIPLE	The past participle of a verb is the form which is used after **to have** in English, eg *ha* **mangiato** *della pasta* (he/she has **eaten** some pasta), *Simona è* **partita** *per Napoli* (Simona has **left** for Naples).
PERSON	In any tense, there are three persons in the singular (1st: *I* ..., 2nd: *you* ..., 3rd: *he/she* ...), and three in the plural (1st: *we* ..., 2nd: *you* ..., 3rd: *they* ...). See also ENDING.
PERSONAL PRONOUNS	Personal pronouns stand for a noun. They usually accompany a verb and can be either the subject (*I*, *you*, *he/she/it*, *we*, *they*) or the object of the verb (*me*, *you*, *him/her/it*, *us*, *them*). Personal pronouns are also commonly used with prepositions (eg *with* **me**, *for* **you**).
PLURAL	See NUMBER.

POSSESSIVE	Possessive adjectives and pronouns are used to indicate possession or ownership. They are words like *my/mine, your/yours, our/ours.*
PREPOSITION	Prepositions are words such as *with, in, to, at.* They are followed by a noun or a pronoun.
PRESENT PARTICIPLE	The present participle is the verb form which ends in **-ing** in English (**-ente/-ante** in Italian).
PRONOUN	A word which stands for a noun. The main categories of pronouns are:

  ★ **Relative pronouns** (eg *who, which, that*)
  ★ **Interrogative pronouns** (eg *who?, what?, which?*)
  ★ **Demonstrative pronouns** (eg *this, that, these*)
  ★ **Possessive pronouns** (eg *mine, yours, his*)
  ★ **Personal pronouns** (eg *you, him, us*)
  ★ **Reflexive pronouns** (eg *myself, himself)*
  ★ **Indefinite pronouns** (eg *something, all*)

QUESTION	There are two question forms: **direct** questions stand on their own and require a question mark at the end (eg *when will he come?*); **indirect** questions are introduced by a clause and require no question mark (eg *I wonder when he will come*).
REFLEXIVE	Reflexive verbs 'reflect' the action back onto the subject (eg *I dressed myself*). They are always found with a reflexive pronoun and are much more common in Italian than in English.
SENTENCE	A sentence is a group of words made up of one or more clauses (see CLAUSE). The end of a sentence is indicated by a punctuation mark (usually a full stop, a question mark or an exclamation mark).
SIMPLE TENSE	Simple tenses are tenses in which the verb consists of one word only, eg *abito, partirà*.
SINGULAR	See NUMBER.
STEM	See VERB STEM.
SUBJECT	The subject of a verb is the noun or pronoun which performs the action. In the sentences *the train left early* and *she bought a record, the train* and *she* are the subjects.

SUBJUNCTIVE   The subjunctive is a verb form which is rarely used in English (eg *if I were you, God save the Queen*), but is common in Italian.

SUPERLATIVE   The form of an adjective or an adverb which, in English, is marked by *the most ..., the ...-est* or *the least ...* .

TENSE   Verbs are used in tenses, which tell us when an action takes place, eg in the present, the past, the future.

VERB   A 'doing' word, which usually describes an action (eg *to sing, to work, to watch*). Some verbs describe a state (eg *to be, to have, to hope*).

VERB STEM   The stem of a verb is its 'basic unit' to which the various endings are added. To find the stem of an Italian verb remove **-are, -ere** or **-ire** from the infinitive.

VOICE   The two voices of a verb are its active and passive forms.

2. ARTICLES

A. THE DEFINITE ARTICLE

1. Forms

In English, there is only one form of the definite article: 'the'. In Italian there are six forms, depending on the gender, the number and the initial letter of the noun following the article:

	SINGULAR	PLURAL
masculine	il	i
	lo (l')	gli
feminine	la (l')	le

Masculine

a) **il/i** are used:

i) before nouns beginning with a consonant:

il libro/i libri　　　　　**il disco/i dischi**
the book/the books　　　　the record/the records

ii) before nouns beginning with **j** (pronounced as in 'jeans'):

il juke-box/i juke-box
the juke-box/the juke-boxes

b) **lo/gli** are used:

i) before nouns beginning with **s** +consonant (**sp, st, sc** etc):

lo studente/gli studenti　　　**lo squalo/gli squali**
the student/the students　　　　the shark/the sharks

lo scultore/gli scultori　　　**lo sciatore/gli sciatore**
the sculptor/the sculptors　　　the skier/the skiers

ii) before **z** and **x**:

lo zio/gli zii
the uncle/the uncles

lo xilofono/gli xilofoni
the xylophone/the xylophones

iii) before **gn, ps**:

> **lo psicologo/gli psicologi**
> the psychologist/the psychologists
>
> **lo gnomo/gli gnomi**
> the gnome/the gnomes

iv) before **i, j** and **y** (all pronounced **i**) + vowel:

> **lo yoghurt/gli yoghurt**
> the yoghurt/the yoghurts
>
> **lo iugoslavo/gli iugoslavi**
> the Yugoslav/the Yugoslavs

c) **l'/gli** are used before words beginning with a vowel:

> **l'albergo/gli alberghi**
> the hotel/the hotels

Feminine

a) **la/le** are used with words beginning with a consonant:

> **la penna/le penne**
> the pen/the pens

b) **l'/le** are used with words beginning with a vowel:

> **l'autostrada/le autostrade**
> the motorway/the motorways
>
> **l'entrata/le entrate**
> the entrance/the entrances

Note: if the noun is preceded by an adjective, the article is placed before the adjective and agrees with it:

> **il bravo studente**
> the good student

Note: if it precedes a foreign word, the article is chosen according to the initial sound in Italian, regardless of spelling:

> **lo champagne**   **lo shampoo**   **il walzer**
> the champagne   the shampoo   the waltz

2. Use

As in English, the definite article is used when referring to something known or given:

> **gli amici di cui ti ho parlato**   **la ragazza di Stefano**
> the friends I told you about   Stefano's girlfriend

However, the definite article is used far more frequently in Italian than in English, in particular in the following cases:

a)   *With uncountable nouns*

> **l'uguaglianza tra gli uomini è un sogno**
> equality among men is a dream

> **l'oro e l'argento sono metalli preziosi**
> gold and silver are precious metals

> **l'italiano non è difficile da imparare**
> Italian is not difficult to learn

> **il verde è il colore della speranza**
> green is the colour of hope

> **il caffè è la bevanda preferita degli Italiani**
> coffee is the Italians' favourite drink

b)   *With nouns indicating categories or species, both singular and plural*

> **il cane è il miglior amico dell'uomo**
> a dog is man's best friend

> **i cani e i gatti sono animali domestici**
> dogs and cats are domestic animals

c)   *With possessives*

> **il tuo vestito è nella mia camera**
> your dress is in my bedroom

Note: the article is not used with the *singular* names of relatives preceded by the possessive adjectives **mio, tuo, suo, nostro** and **vostro** (all but **loro**):

> **mio padre**   **tua madre**
> my father   your mother

But: **il loro padre**   **le mie sorelle**
> their father   my sisters

The article is used in familiar expressions and with diminutives:

> **la mia mamma**   **la nostra sorellina**
> my mummy   our little sister

See also pp 83-7.

d) *With geographical nouns except for towns and several islands*

l'Italia ha la forma di uno stivale
Italy is the shape of a boot

l'Arno passa per Firenze
the river Arno flows through Florence

Venezia è una città romantica
Venice is a romantic city

Capri e Ischia sono due piccole isole
Capri and Ischia are two small islands

But:

i) articles are used when towns and some islands are accompanied by an adjective or by a complement:

la bella Capri   **la Venezia dei Dogi**
beautiful Capri   the Venice of the Doges

ii) when a country, region or continent is preceded by 'in', it does not take the article, provided that it is not plural or accompanied by an adjective or a complement:

vado in Sicilia   **mi piacerebbe vivere in Francia**
I'm going to Sicily   I'd like to live in France

iii) **Andorra, Gibilterra** (Gibraltar), **Monaco, Panama, Israele** and **San Marino** never take the article:

San Marino è la repubblica più piccola del mondo
San Marino is the smallest republic in the world

e) *With certain expressions of time*

il 1968 fu un anno difficile
1968 was a difficult year

sono le tre
it's three o'clock

f) *With certain expressions of quantity*

il due per cento
two per cent

40 km all'ora (**all'** = a *preposition* + **l'** *article*)
40 km per hour

20.000 lire all'ora (**all'** = a *preposition* + **l'** *article*)
20,000 lire an hour

5.000 lire al chilo (**al** = **a** *preposition* + **il** *article*)
5,000 lire a kilo

g) *With titles*

il signor Bianchi   **il dottor Franchi**
Mr Bianchi   Dr Franchi

But: it is not used in direct speech:

"Buon giorno, professor Bianchi"
'Good morning, Professor Bianchi'

B.   THE INDEFINITE ARTICLE

1.   Forms

The forms of the indefinite article are the same as those of the numeral **uno** (one):

vuoi un libro?   do you want a book
                           do you want one book?

masculine	**un**
	uno
feminine	**una**
	un'

Masculine

a)   **un** is used before words beginning with a consonant or a vowel:

un libro   **un albergo**
a book   a hotel

b)   **uno** is used before words beginning with **s** + consonant, before **z, x, gn, ps,** and before **i, j** and **y** (all pronounced **i**) + vowel:

uno studente   **uno iugoslavo**
a student   a Yugoslav

uno gnomo   **uno psicologo**
a gnome   a psychologist

uno zio   **uno yoghurt**
an uncle   a yoghurt

Feminine

a)   **una** is used before words beginning with a consonant and with **i** +
     another vowel:

una strada	**una iugoslava**
a road	a Yugoslav woman

b)   **un'** is used before vowels:

un'autostrada	**un'amica**
a motorway	a friend (*fem*)

But: **un amico**
         a friend (*masc*)

Note: if the noun is preceded by an adjective, the article is placed
          before the adjective and agrees with it:

un bravo studente
a good student

Note: if it precedes foreign words, the article is chosen according to the
          initial sound in Italian, regardless of spelling:

uno shampoo	**un walzer**
a shampoo	a waltz

Plural

un/uno/una/un' have no plural form, although they could be substituted
by the partitive articles (see p 22) or by the adjectives **qualche, alcuni/e**
(see pp 89-92).

2.   Use

As in English, the indefinite article is used when referring to something indefinite:

uno studente	**una scala**
a student	a ladder

However, the indefinite article is used far more frequently in Italian
than in English, in particular in the following cases:

a)   *With uncountable nouns*

ci vuole una grande pazienza per fare questo lavoro
great patience is required to do this job

questo è un alluminio molto resistente
this is very strong aluminium

ha una bellezza straordinaria
she has extraordinary beauty

b) *With approximate numbers* (see also chapter 10, pp 219-20)

una decina   **un centinaio**
about ten   about a hundred

c) *To convey a sense of indeterminacy*

ho camminato per un tre chilometri
I walked for about three kilometres

Note: **che ragazza graziosa!**
what a nice girl!

un chilo e mezzo
a kilo and a half

C.   THE PARTITIVE ARTICLE

The Italian partitive article corresponds to 'some'/'any' in English.

1.   Forms

The partitive article is formed by combining the preposition **di** with
the definite article:

MASCULINE		FEMININE	
SINGULAR			
di + il	= del	di + la	= della
di + lo	= dello	di + l'	= dell'
di + l'	= dell'		
PLURAL			
di + i	= dei	di + le	= delle
di + gli	= degli		

Note: like definite articles, partitive articles are chosen according to the
gender, the number and the initial letter of the noun which follows (see p 16):

del vino   **dello zucchero**   **dell'olio**
some wine   some sugar   some oil

della carta   **dell'acqua**
some paper   some water

dei libri	**degli errori**	**delle lettere**
some books	some mistakes	some letters

2. Use

a) *Singular*

This is only used with uncountable nouns both in affirmative and interrogative sentences:

ho comprato del pane	**incontrai della gente**
I've bought some bread	I met some people
volete del burro?	**avete della farina?**
do you want some butter?	do you have any flour?

b) *Plural*

This is used both in affirmative and interrogative sentences:

vorrei delle arance	**ha lasciato delle impronte**
I'd like some oranges	he/she left some fingerprints
comprammo degli spinaci	**hai incontrato del ragazzi simpatici?**
we bought some spinach	did you meet some nice boys?

3. Omission

a) In Italian it is possible to omit the partitive article more often than in English, especially when the idea of quantity is not important to the speaker:

c'era polvere dappertutto
there was dust everywhere

avete latte scremato?
do you have any skimmed milk?

abbiamo mangiato patatine fritte
we ate chips

affittano appartamenti per l'estate
they rent out flats for the summer

avete scarpe di pelle?
do you have any leather shoes?

b) In particular, the partitive article is omitted:

i) *always* in negative sentences:

non ho amici	**non c'è pane**
I've no friends	there isn't any bread

ii) *always* after the preposition **di**:

a casa di amici
at friends'

ho voglia di fragole
I would like (some) strawberries

iii) *preferably* after other prepositions:

rispose con parole gentili
he/she replied with kind words

una torta con fragole
a cake with strawberries

4. Alternatives

a) **qualche** (some/any) is used only with singular, countable nouns although there is a plural sense:

ho letto qualche racconto di Calvino
I read some short stories by Calvino

b) **un po' di** (a little/some/any) can be used as an alternative to both singular and sometimes plural partitive articles:

vuoi un po' di latte?
would you like some milk?

vorrei un po' di fragole
I'd like some strawberries

c) **alcuni/e** (some/a few) can be used as an alternative to the plural partitive article:

ho fatto alcuni esercizi di grammatica
I did some grammar exercises

d) **nessun(o)/nessuna** or **alcun(o)/alcuna** (no/not any) can be used before countable nouns but only in the singular:

non ho letto nessun libro di Moravia
non ho letto alcun libro di Moravia
I haven't read any book(s) by Moravia

qui non c'è nessuna penna che funzioni
qui non c'è alcuna penna che funzioni
there's no pen here that works

3. NOUNS

Nouns are naming words, which refer to persons, animals, things, places or abstract ideas.

A. GENDER

All Italian nouns are masculine or feminine; there is no neuter as in English. Although no absolute rule can be stated, the gender can often be determined either by the *meaning* or the *ending* of the noun.

1. By meaning

Masculine

a) *Names of male people and animals*

l'uomo	**il padre**	**il cane**
the man	the father	the dog
il ragazzo	**il leone**	**il gatto**
the boy	the lion	the cat

Note:

i) there are some nouns denoting people which, although feminine in gender, refer to a man or could be used when referring to both a woman and a man:

la guardia	**la spia**	**la guida**
the guard	the spy	the guide
la vittima	**la persona**	
the victim	the person	

ii) there are some nouns denoting animals which, although feminine in gender, refer both to male and female animals (see also p 27):

la giraffa	**la pantera**	**la tigre**
the giraffe	the panther	the tiger

b) *Languages*

l'italiano	**il francese**	**lo spagnolo**
Italian	French	Spanish

c) *Names of common trees and shrubs*

il melo the apple tree	**il pino** the pine tree	**il biancospino** the hawthorn
il pioppo the poplar	**il noce** the walnut tree	**il castagno** the chestnut tree

But: **la betulla** **la palma** **la quercia**
the birch the palm tree the oak

d) *Names of mountains, rivers, lakes, seas, oceans*

gli Appennini the Appennines	**il Monte Bianco** Mont-Blanc	**l'Arno** the Arno
il Garda Lake Garda	**l'Adriatico** the Adriatic sea	**il Pacifico** the Pacific Ocean

But: **le Alpi** **le Dolomiti** **la Senna**
the Alps the Dolomites the Seine

e) *Cardinal points*

il nord the north	**il sud** the south	**l'est** the east	**l'ovest** the west

il meridione the South	**il ponente** the West

f) *Names of months and days*

gennaio January	**marzo** March	**il lunedì** Monday	**il sabato** Saturday

But: **la domenica**
Sunday

g) *Metals and chemical elements*

l'oro gold	**il ferro** iron	**l'ottone** brass
il carbone coal	**l'ossigeno** oxygen	**l'uranio** uranium

h) *Colours*

il bianco white	**il rosso** red	**il verde** green

Feminine

a) *Names of female people and animals*

la donna	**la madre**	**la gatta**
the woman	the mother	the she-cat

Note:

i) there are some nouns denoting people which, although masculine in gender, generally refer to women, although they could also refer to men (see p 31):

il soprano	**il contralto**
the soprano	the contralto

ii) there are some nouns denoting animals which, although masculine in gender, can refer both to male and female animals (see also p 25):

il leopardo	**il corvo**	**lo scimpanzè**
the leopard	the raven	the chimpanzee

b) *Names of fruit and nuts*

la mela	**la pera**	**l'uva**
the apple	the pear	the grapes
la ciliegia	**l'arancia**	**la noce**
the cherry	the orange	the walnut

But:

il limone	**il melone**	**il pompelmo**
the lemon	the melon	the grapefruit

c) *Continents*

l'Europa	**l'America**	**l'Australia**
Europe	America	Australia

d) *Countries*

l'Italia	**la Francia**	**la Gran Bretagna**
Italy	France	Great Britain
l'Argentina	**la Germania**	**la Danimarca**
Argentina	Germany	Denmark

But: there are several exceptions:

il Belgio	**il Canada**	**l'Egitto**
Belgium	Canada	Egypt
il Giappone	**il Portogallo**	**gli Stati Uniti**
Japan	Portugal	the United States

e) *Names of islands*

la Sicilia	la Sardegna	l'Elba	le Canarie
Sicily	Sardinia	Elba	the Canaries

But:

il Madagascar		il Borneo
Madagascar		Borneo

f) *Cities and towns*

Torino	Milano	Venezia	Mosca
Turin	Milan	Venice	Moscow

But:

il Cairo
Cairo

g) *Many abstract nouns*

la bontà	la libertà	la virtù
goodness	freedom	virtue

la chimica	la pace	la giustizia
chemistry	peace	justice

But:

l'amore (*masc*)	l'egoismo (*masc*)	il coraggio
love	egoism	courage

2. By ending

a) Almost all nouns ending in **-o** are masculine:

il quadro	il prezzo	il libro
the picture	the price	the book

But: there are a few exceptions:

la mano	la radio	la dinamo
the hand	the radio	the dynamo

la foto	la moto
the photo	the motorbike

Note: **eco** 'echo' is both masculine and feminine in the singular, but it is always masculine in the plural (**echi**).

b) Most nouns ending in **-a** are feminine:

la casa	la sedia	la pianta
the house	the chair	the plant

But: there are several masculine nouns ending in **-a** (mostly derived from Greek):

il profeta the prophet	**il dramma** the drama	**il problema** the problem
il tema the theme	**il poeta** the poet	**il papa** the pope

Note: there are also some nouns ending in **-cida** and **-ista** which can be either gender:

il giornalista the journalist (*male*)	**la giornalista** the journalist (*female*)
un artista an artist (*male*)	**un'artista** an artist (*female*)
un omicida a murderer	**un'omicida** a murderess

c) Nouns ending in **-e** can be either masculine or feminine:

la notte the night	**la ragione** the reason	**la mente** the mind
il fiume the river	**il dente** the tooth	**il ponte** the bridge

i) however, most nouns ending in **-zione**, **-sione**, **-gione**, **-udine**, **-ite**, **-igine** and those in **-ice** referring to women are feminine:

la soluzione the solution	**la conclusione** the conclusion
la regione the region	**l'abitudine** the habit
l'appendicite the appendicitis	**l'origine** the origin
la scrittrice the woman writer	

ii) most nouns ending in **-ore**, **-ere**, **-ame**, **-ale**, **-ile** are masculine:

il motore the engine	**il carcere** the prison
il bestiame the cattle	**il temporale** the storm
il canile the kennel	

Note: nouns ending in **-e** which indicate titles (**signore, professore, ingegnere, ragioniere,** etc) drop their final **-e** before names and surnames:

il signor Rossi	**il professor Bianchi**
Mr Rossi	Professor Bianchi

d)   Most nouns ending in **-i** are feminine:

la crisi	**la tesi**	**l'analisi**
the crisis	the thesis	the analysis

But: **il brindisi**
the toast

e)   Nouns ending in **-u** can be either feminine or masculine:

la virtù	**il bambù**
virtue	bamboo

f)   Nouns ending with a consonant (foreign words, for the most part) are masculine:

lo sport	**il film**	**il tram**
sport	the film	the tram

But:

la hall	**la star**
the hall	the star

B.   THE FORMATION OF FEMININES

1.   The feminine equivalent of most masculine nouns ending in **-o** and **-e** is formed by substituting these endings with **-a**:

il bambino	**la bambina**	little boy/girl
il cavallo	**la cavalla**	horse/mare
l'infermiere	**l'infermiera**	male/female nurse
il cameriere	**la cameriera**	waiter/waitress

2.   The feminine equivalent of some masculine nouns ending in **-o, -e** and **-a** is formed by adding **-essa** to their stem:

il campione	**la campionessa**	male/female champion
il leone	**la leonessa**	lion/lioness
il poeta	**la poetessa**	poet/poetess
il professore	**la professoressa**	male/female professor

3. With masculine nouns ending in **-tore**, the ending changes to **-trice** to form the feminine equivalent:

il pittore	**la pittrice**	male/female painter
il vincitore	**la vincitrice**	male/female winner
l'imperatore	**l'imperatrice**	emperor/empress
l'attore	**l'attrice**	actor/actress
lo scrittore	**la scrittrice**	male/female writer

But: **il dottore** **la dottoressa** male/female doctor

4. Some nouns have a common gender, that is to say, they have the same endings for the masculine and the feminine. They can be distinguished by the article or by the adjective which accompanies them. See also (p 29):

a) Some nouns ending in **-e**:

il cantante	**la cantante**	male/female singer
il nipote	**la nipote**	nephew/niece
un agente	**un'agente**	male/female agent
un amante	**un'amante**	male/female lover

Note: these nouns have the same endings in the masculine and feminine plurals (see p 37):

i cantanti **le cantanti** male/female singers

b) All nouns ending in **-ista** and **-cida**:

il pianista	**la pianista**	male/female pianist
un artista	**un'artista**	male/female artist
il suicida	**la suicida**	male/female suicide
un omicida	**un'omicida**	murderer/murderess

Note: these nouns have different endings for the masculine and feminine plurals (see p 36):

i pianisti **le pianiste** male/female pianists

c) Some nouns derived from Greek, ending in **-a**:

il collega	**la collega**	male/female colleague
un atleta	**un'atleta**	male/female athlete
il pediatra	**la pediatra**	male/female paediatrician

Note: these nouns have different endings for the masculine and feminine plurals (see p 35):

gli atleti **le atlete** male/female athletes

Note: the gender of articles and adjectives should agree with the gender of these nouns:

un cantante famoso
a well-known singer (*male*)

una cantante famosa
a well-known singer (*female*)

un bravo giornalista
a good journalist (*male*)

una brava giornalista
a good journalist (*female*)

5.   Some nouns indicating professions or positions are used in the masculine to refer to women as well, since their regular feminine form would give the noun an ironic or pejorative significance:

il medico	doctor
l'avvocato	lawyer
il ministro	minister

6.   Some names of animals are only masculine or feminine and their feminine and masculine equivalents can be formed either by adding the words **femmina/maschio** or by placing the expressions **la femmina del/il maschio della** in front of the noun in question:

il leopardo
the leopard

il leopardo femmina/la femmina del leopardo
the female leopard

la giraffa
the giraffe

la giraffa maschio/il maschio della giraffa
the male giraffe

7.   Irregular feminines

il dio	**la dea**	god/goddess
lo stregone	**la strega**	wizard/witch
l'eroe	**l'eroina**	hero/heroine
il re	**la regina**	king/queen
lo zar	**la zarina**	tsar/tsarina
il gallo	**la gallina**	cock/hen

8.   The feminine form of masculine nouns for names of trees refers to the fruit of the respective tree:

il melo	**la mela**	apple tree/apple
il pero	**la pera**	pear tree/pear

9.   Nouns having only one gender - either masculine or feminine - which could refer to both sexes:

una persona
a person (*male/female*)

la sentinella
the sentry (*male/female*)

la spia
the spy (*male/female*)

il soprano
the soprano (*female/male*)

un medico
a doctor (*male/female*)

il ministro
the minister (*male/female*)

mio padre è una persona straordinaria
my father is an extraordinary person

Maria è un bravo medico
Maria is a good doctor

la tigre addomesticata
the tame tiger

10. Some nouns change their meaning according to gender, but their endings do not change:

il fine aim	**la fine** end
il radio radium	**la radio** radio
il capitale capital (*money*)	**la capitale** capital (*town*)
il fronte front	**la fronte** forehead

C. THE FORMATION OF PLURALS

1. Nouns in ending in *-o*

a) Masculine nouns ending in **-o** change to **-i**:

il libro	i libri	book
il sasso	i sassi	stone
il tavolo	i tavoli	table
il gatto	i gatti	cat

Note: some nouns ending in **-o**, although changing to **-i** for the plural, also change their stem:

il dio	gli dei	god
il tempio	i templi	temple
l'uomo	gli uomini	man

b) Feminine nouns ending in **-o** remain unchanged in the plural (see also p 38):

la moto	**le moto**	motorbike
la foto	**le foto**	photo

But: **la mano** **le mani** hand

c) Nouns ending in **-io** with an unstressed **-i-** change to **-i**:

l'esempio	**gli esempi**	example
l'occhio	**gli occhi**	eye
il figlio	**i figli**	son

Note: some nouns ending in **-io** can be confused in the plural with nouns which have a different meaning but the same spelling. In these cases an accent or a double **i** can be used to differentiate them:

il principe	**i principi**	prince
	i prìncipi	
il principio	**i principi**	principle
	i princìpi	
	i princîpi	
	i principii	

d) Nouns ending in **-io** with a stressed **-i-** change to **-ii**:

lo zio	**gli zii**	uncle
il pendio	**i pendii**	slope
il mormorio	**i mormorii**	murmur

e) Nouns ending in **-co** and **-go** change to **-chi, -ci, -ghi** and **-gi** in the plural but follow no absolute rule. However, there are two main categories:

i) if the stress falls on the penultimate syllable, the ending changes to **-chi** and **-ghi**, although there are various exceptions:

il cuoco	**i cuochi**	cook
il fuoco	**i fuochi**	fire
l'albergo	**gli alberghi**	hotel
il fungo	**i funghi**	mushroom

But: **l'amico** **gli amici** friend

il porco **i porci** pig

ii) if the stress falls before the penultimate syllable, the ending changes to **-ci** and **-gi**, although there are various exceptions:

il medico	i medici	doctor
il portico	i portici	porch
il teologo	i teologi	theologian
l'asparago	gli asparagi	asparagus

But:

il carico	i carichi	load
l'obbligo	gli obblighi	obligation

Note: some nouns have a plural both in **-ci/-gi** and **-chi/-ghi**:

il manico	i manici/i manichi	handle

Note: nouns ending in **-logo** generally change to **-logi** if they refer to people, and **-loghi** if they refer to things:

lo psicologo	gli psicologi	psychologist
l'archeologo	gli archeologi	archaeologist
il dialogo	i dialoghi	dialogue
il catalogo	i cataloghi	catalogue

f) Some masculine nouns ending in **-o** change gender in the plural and their ending becomes **-a** (see p 38):

il centinaio	le centinaia	about a hundred
l'uovo	le uova	egg

2. Nouns ending in *-a*

a) Feminine nouns ending in **-a** change to **-e**:

la casa	le case	house
la ragazza	le ragazze	girl
la leonessa	le leonesse	lioness

But: **arma** and **ala** are exceptions as their endings change to **-i**:

l'arma	le armi	weapon
l'ala	le ali	wing

b) Masculine nouns ending in **-a** (mostly of Greek origin) change to **-i**:

il problema	i problemi	problem
il clima	i climi	climate
il fantasma	i fantasmi	ghost
l'atleta	gli atleti	athlete
il papa	i papi	pope
il pigiama	i pigiami	pyjamas

Note: some nouns ending in **-a** change to **-i** in the plural if they refer to men and **-e** if they refer to women:

i) nouns ending in **-ista** and **-cida**:

l'artista	gli artisti	artist *(male)*
l'artista	le artiste	*(female)*
l'omicida	gli omicidi	murderer
l'omicida	le omicide	murderess

ii) some nouns of Greek origin:

il collega	i colleghi	male colleague
la collega	le colleghe	female colleague

Note: some masculine nouns in **-a** do not change in the plural (see also p 38):

il boa	i boa	boa

c) Nouns ending in **-ca** and **-ga** change to **-che** and **-ghe** if feminine and **-chi** and **-ghi** if masculine:

la banca	le banche	bank
la piaga	le piaghe	wound, scar
il monarca	i monarchi	monarch
lo stratega	gli strateghi	strategist

d) Nouns ending in **-cia** and **-gia** change to **-ce** and **-ge** if the ending is preceded by a consonant, and to **-cie** and **-gie** if it is preceded by a vowel:

la bilancia	le bilance	scales
la pioggia	le piogge	rain
la camicia	le camicie	shirt
la valigia	le valigie	suitcase

e) Nouns ending in **-ia**, **-cia**, **-gia**, **-scia** with the **-i-** stressed retain the **-i-** in the plural:

la galleria	le gallerie	gallery
la farmacia	le farmacie	chemist's
la bugia	le bugie	lie
la scia	le scie	trail

f) Nouns ending in **-ea** change to **-ee**, whether the **-e-** is stressed or not:

l'assemblea	le assemblee	assembly

3. Nouns ending in -e

a) Both masculine and feminine nouns change from **-e** to **-i**:

il fiore	i fiori	flower
la cornice	le cornici	frame

Note: il bue   i buoi   ox

b) Nouns having the same ending for masculine and feminine in the singular, also have the same ending in the plural;

il nipote	i nipoti	nephew
la nipote	le nipoti	niece

4. Nouns which do not change in the plural

a) Nouns ending in **-i**:

la crisi	le crisi	crisis
l'alibi	gli alibi	alibi

b) Nouns ending in **-u**:

la virtù	le virtù	virtue
il bambù	i bambù	bamboo

c) Nouns ending in **-ie**:

la serie	le serie	series

But: the following nouns are exceptions:

la superficie	le superfici	surface
la moglie	le mogli	wife
l'effigie	le effigi	effigy

d) Nouns ending in an accented vowel:

la città	le città	town
l'università	le università	university
il caffè	i caffè	coffee
il lunedì	i lunedì	Monday

e) Nouns of foreign origin ending in a consonant:

il club	i club	
il film	i film	
lo sport	gli sport	

f) Acronyms:

due BMW	**molte Fiat**	
two BMWs	a lot of Fiats	

g) Nouns which have only one syllable:

il re	**i re**	king
lo sci	**gli sci**	ski

h) A few masculine nouns ending in -a:

il cinema	**i cinema**	cinema
il vaglia	**i vaglia**	money order
il sosia	**i sosia**	double

i) Feminine nouns ending in -o:

la biro	**le biro**	biro
l'auto	**le auto**	car
la foto	**le foto**	photo
la radio	**le radio**	radio
la moto	**le moto**	motorbike
But: **la mano**	**le mani**	hand

5. Irregularities

a) A few nouns change gender in the plural and have the ending -a:

il paio	**le paia**	pair
il riso	**le risa**	laugh
l'uovo	**le uova**	egg
il centinaio	**le centinaia**	hundred
il migliaio	**le migliaia**	thousand
il miglio	**le miglia**	mile
Also: **il carcere**	**le carceri**	prison

b) A few nouns are used only in the plural:

   i) nouns indicating pairs of things:

i calzoni	trousers
le forbici	scissors
gli occhiali	spectacles

   ii) nouns referring to words which have a plural sense:

i viveri	provisions
i dintorni	surroundings

iii)   other nouns:

le nozze	wedding
le tenebre	darkness

c)   Some nouns are used only in the singular, since, as in English, they do not have a plural:

la chimica	chemistry
il tifo	typhus
il rame	copper
il latte	milk

d)   A few nouns have two plurals, each with a different meaning:

il braccio	arm
le braccia	arms
i bracci	the arms of a cross etc
il labbro	lip
le labbra	lips
i labbri	the lips (opening) of a wound etc
il muro	wall
le mura	the walls of a city
i muri	the walls of a house
l'osso	bone
le ossa	the bones of a human skeleton
gli ossi	the bones for a dog etc

e)   A few nouns have two plurals without any difference in meaning:

il ginocchio	knee
le ginocchia	
i ginocchi	
il lenzuolo	sheet
le lenzuola	
i lenzuoli	
il grido	shout
le grida	
i gridi	

f)   A few nouns have two plurals and two singulars:

l'orecchio	ear
l'orecchia	
gli orecchi	
le orecchie	

l'arancio	orange
l'arancia	
gli aranci	
le arance	

6. Compound nouns

Compound nouns generally behave like ordinary nouns in the plural (ie changing the end vowel). However in some cases both elements remain unchanged, and in other cases the first element changes. In particular:

a) Nouns made up of *noun + noun* generally change their end vowel:

il pescecane	i pescecani	shark
la madreperla	le madreperle	mother-of-pearl

Note:

 i) feminine nouns containing the word **capo** remain unchanged in the plural:

la caposquadra	le caposquadra	forewoman

 ii) masculine nouns containing the word **capo** can have various plurals and should be checked individually in a dictionary:

il capostazione	i capistazione	station master
il capolavoro	i capolavori	masterpiece

b) Nouns made up of *adjective + noun* change the end vowel:

il bassorilievo	i bassorilievi	bas-relief
l'altoparlante	gli altoparlanti	loudspeaker

But:

la mezzaluna	le mezzelune	half-moon
il purosangue	i purosangue	thoroughbred

c) Nouns made up of *noun + adjective* change the end vowel of both noun and adjective:

la cassaforte	le casseforti	safe
la terracotta	le terrecotte	terracotta

But:

il palcoscenico	i palcoscenici	stage

d) Nouns made up of *verb + noun*:

 i) nouns made up of *verb + singular feminine noun* do not change in the plural:

il cacciavite	i cacciavite	screwdriver
il portacenere	i portacenere	ashtray

But: l'asciugamano   gli asciugamani   towel

ii)   nouns made up of *verb + singular masculine noun* change the end vowel in the plural:

il parafango	i parafanghi	mudguard
il passaporto	i passaporti	passport

iii)   nouns made up of *verb + plural noun* remain unchanged:

l'apriscatole	gli apriscatole	tin-opener
l'attaccapanni	gli attaccapanni	hanger

e)   Nouns made up of *verb + verb* do not change in the plural:

il saliscendi	i saliscendi	latch

f)   Nouns made up of *adverb + verb* do not change in the plural:

il benestare	i benestare	approval

g)   Nouns made up of either a *preposition* or an *adverb + noun* can have various plurals and should be checked individually in a dictionary:

il senzatetto	i senzatetto	homeless person
il benefattore	i benefattori	benefactor
la contrabbasso	i contrabbassi	(double) bass
il soprannome	i soprannomi	nickname

h)   When two nouns are separated by a hyphen, only the first noun changes:

il divano-letto	i divani-letto	sofa-bed

7.   Collective nouns

a)   Singular nouns in Italian, but plural in English:

la gente	people
la polizia	police
il bestiame	cattle

la polizia *ha* arrestato il ladro
the police have arrested the thief

b) Plural nouns in Italian, but singular in English:

le notizie	news
i mobili	furniture
gli spaghetti	spaghetti

sono buone notizie
that's good news

questi spaghetti sono buoni
this spaghetti's great

8. Proper nouns

a) Ordinary family names are invariable in the plural:

ho incontrato i (signori) Bragato alla festa
I met the Bragatos at the party

b) For some historical names add **-i** for the plural:

i Borboni the Bourbons

D. SUFFIXES

In Italian the meaning of some nouns (and also of adjectives and adverbs) can be altered through the addition of suffixes (different endings) which add different shades of meaning:

a) The suffixes **-ino/a**, **-etto/a**, **-ello/a**, **-ellino/a** are generally diminutives:

ragazzo	**ragazzino**
boy	small boy
casa	**casetta**
house	pretty little house
secchio	**secchiello**
bucket	small bucket
rosa	**rosellina**
rose	lovely little rose

b) The suffixes **-one/a** increase the idea of size or strengthen the meaning of the original word:

ragazzo	**ragazzone**
boy	big boy

c) The suffixes **-astro/a**, **-accio/a**, **-attolo/a**, **-ucolo/a**, **-upolo/a** give the noun negative connotations:

poeta	**poetastro**
poet	bad poet
ragazzo	**ragazzaccio**
boy	bad boy
uomo	**omiciattolo**
man	worthless/small, ugly man
professore	**professorucolo**
teacher	mediocre teacher
casa	**casupola**
house	wretched house

Note: it is important to remember that a lot of words ending in these suffixes have separate meanings, and that not every word can be altered in the way described above:

posta	**postino**
mail/post-office	postman
borsa	**borsetta**
bag	handbag
carta	**cartone**
paper	cardboard

E. USE OF CAPITAL LETTERS

There are some differences in the use of capital letters between English and Italian. Capitals are not used in Italian for:

a) *Nationalities*

> **un italiano e un inglese**
> an Italian and an Englishman

Note: plural nouns indicating a race can be capitalized in Italian:

> **gli Americani**
> Americans

But: the plural adjective is never capitalized:

> **i soldati americani**
> American soldiers

b)   *Inhabitants of towns* (both nouns and adjectives)

una fiorentina a Florentine	**un londinese** a Londoner

c)   *Languages*

studio il francese
I'm studying French

d)   *Months and days of the week*

aprile April	**sabato** Saturday

e)   *Kings, popes, bishops etc*

la regina Elisabetta
Queen Elizabeth

f)   *san/santa/santo referring to a saint*

san Marco Saint Mark	**sant'Anna** Saint Anne

But: it is capitalized when it refers to the name of a church

la basilica di San Marco
the basilica of Saint Mark

4. ADJECTIVES

Adjectives are variable parts of speech which accompany a noun to describe its qualities or to define it better:

un ristorante italiano
an Italian restaurant

un celebre ballerino
a famous dancer

una spiaggia affollata
a crowded beach

un'avventura emozionante
an exciting adventure

A. AGREEMENT OF ADJECTIVES

In Italian adjectives agree in gender and number with the noun they qualify. This means that, unlike English adjectives, which don't change, Italian adjectives have different forms which are determined by the noun they go with:

il vestito *rosso*
the red dress

i fiori *rossi*
the red flowers

la camicia *rossa*
the red shirt

le matite *rosse*
the red pencils

Note:

i) when two or more singular words share the same adjective, this adjective will be in the plural:

una chiesa e una piazza moderne
a modern church and square

ii) if one of these words is masculine, the adjective will be masculine plural:

il ragazzo e la ragazza cinesi
the Chinese boy and girl

una gonna, una giacca e un cappello neri
a black skirt, jacket and hat

iii) however, if the adjective precedes the series of nouns, it agrees with the nearest one:

belle ville e castelli
beautiful villas and castles

bei parchi e fontane
beautiful parks and fountains

B. THE FORMATION OF FEMININES

1. Adjectives ending in **-o** form their feminine in **-a**:

    un bambino contento   **una bambina contenta**
    a happy boy   a happy girl

2. Adjectives ending in **-e** do not change in the feminine:

    un esercizio difficile   **una lezione difficile**
    a difficult exercise   a difficult lesson

3. Adjectives ending in **-tore** have their feminine equivalent in **-trice**, as with nouns (see p 31):

    il gruppo vincitore   **la squadra vincitrice**
    the winning group   the winning team

4. Adjectives ending in **-ista** and **-cida** have the same endings for the masculine and the feminine (see p 31):

    un ragazzo egoista   **una ragazza egoista**
    a selfish boy   a selfish girl

5. Adjectives of foreign origin do not have a feminine form:

    un cielo blu   **una maglia blu**
    a blue sky   a blue jumper

C. THE FORMATION OF PLURALS

1. Adjectives ending in **-o** and **-a** have plural forms in **-i** for the masculine and **-e** for the feminine:

    degli uomini anziani   **delle donne anziane**
    some old men   some old women

2. Adjectives ending in **-e** have plural forms in **-i**:

    dei prati verdi   **delle valli verdi**
    some green meadows   some green valleys

3. Adjectives with other endings:

For the formation of plurals, adjectives follow the same rules given for the plural of nouns (see p 33):

a) Masculine forms of adjectives ending in **-io** with stressed **-i**:

pio	→	**pii**	pious

b) Masculine forms of adjectives ending in **-io** with unstressed **-i**:

ampio	→	**ampi**	ample

c) Masculine forms of adjectives ending in **-co** and **-go** with the stress on the penultimate syllable:

stanco	→	**stanchi**	tired
lungo	→	**lunghi**	long
But: **amico**	→	**amici**	friendly
greco	→	**greci**	Greek

d) Masculine forms of adjectives ending in **-co** and **-go** with the stress before the penultimate syllable:

magnifico	→	**magnifici**	magnificent
But: **carico**	→	**carichi**	loaded, laden

e) Feminine forms of adjectives ending in **-ca**, **-ga**:

antica	→	**antiche**	ancient, antique
larga	→	**larghe**	wide

f) Feminine forms of adjectives in **-cia**, **-gia** preceded by a consonant:

spilorcia	→	**spilorce**	stingy

g) Feminine forms of adjectives in **-cia**, **-gia** preceded by a vowel:

randagia	→	**randagie**	stray

h) Adjectives having a common gender ending in **-a** for the singular, including those ending in **-ista** and **-cida**:

belga (*masc*) →	**belgi**	Belgian
belga (*fem*) →	**belghe**	

4. Adjectives which do not change in the plural:

a) Adjectives ending in **-i**:

un numero pari	**i numeri pari**
an even number	even numbers
un numero dispari	**i numeri dispari**
an odd number	odd numbers

b) Adjectives of foreign origin:

il vestito blu	**le calze blu**
the blue dress	the blue socks
il concerto rock	**i concerti rock**
the rock concert	the rock concerts

c) Some adjectives of colour which were originally nouns in their own right:

le tende crema	**gli ombretti viola**
the cream curtains	the purple eyeshadows
le tute rosa	**gli stivali marrone**
the pink overalls	the brown boots

Note: modified expressions of colour do not change in the plural either:

i maglioni verde acqua
the bluish green jumpers

i rossetti rosso ciliegia
the cherry red lipsticks

although **verde** and **rosso** by themselves behave as regular adjectives.

D.   IRREGULAR ADJECTIVES

1. **bello** (beautiful), when it precedes the noun it qualifies, has forms similar to those of the definite article (see p 16):

	SINGULAR	PLURAL
masculine	**bello**	**begli**
	bell'	
	bel	**bei**
feminine	**bella**	**belle**
	bell'	

un bel prato a beautiful meadow	**un bell'albero** a beautiful tree
dei begli occhi beautiful eyes	**dei bei giardini** beautiful gardens
una bella donna a beautiful woman	**delle belle ragazze** some beautiful girls

But: when it follows the noun, it retains its regular forms
bello/bella/belli/belle:

un ragazzo bello a handsome boy	**una ragazza bella** a beautiful girl
i ragazzi belli the handsome boys	**le ragazze belle** the beautiful girls

Note: the demonstrative adjective **quello** follows the same pattern as
bello (see pp 92-3).

2. **buono** (good) in the singular, when it precedes the noun it qualifies,
    has forms similar to those of the indefinite article (see p 20):

un buon pranzo a good dinner	**un buono stipendio** a good salary	**un buon amico** a good friend
una buona cucina good cooking	**una buon'amica/una buona amica** a good friend	

Note: the plural is regular - **buoni, buone**:

dei buoni amici (some) good friends (*masc*)	**delle buone amiche** (some) good friends (*fem*)

3. **grande** (great, big) can be shortened to **gran** before a noun
    beginning with a consonant other than **z** or **s** + consonant, **gn**,
    ps or **x**:

un gran pasticcio	a great mess
una gran piazza	a big square
una grande occasione	a great opportunity
un grande sciocco	a great fool

However, in most cases, **gran** can be replaced by **grande**:

un gran successo **un grande successo**	a great success

Note: **grande** can be shortened to **grand'** before a noun beginning with
a vowel, but **grande** can also be used and it is more common:

un grand'aiuto **un grande aiuto**	a great help

But: it is shortened when used as an intensifier:

fa un gran caldo oggi
it is extremely hot today

4.   santo (Saint):

i)   shortened to **sant'** before male and female names beginning with a vowel:

| **sant'Ambrogio** | Saint Ambrose |
| **sant'Anna** | Saint Anne |

ii)   shortened to **san** before male names beginning with a consonant other than s + consonant:

| **san Pietro** | Saint Peter |
| **san Zaccaria** | Saint Zachariah |

iii)   used in full, **santo**, before male names beginning with s followed by a consonant:

| **santo Stefano** | Saint Stephen |

iv)   used in full in the feminine form, **santa**, before female names beginning with a consonant:

| **santa Chiara** | Saint Clare |

Note: frequent anomalies are found in place names:

San Stino

E.   POSITION OF ADJECTIVES

1.   In Italian, adjectives usually follow the nouns they qualify:

| **una pizza magnifica** | **un discorso interessante** |
| a magnificent pizza | an interesting speech |

2.   However the following common adjectives usually precede the noun:

antico	ancient, antique	**giovane**	young
bello	beautiful	**grande**	great
breve	short	**largo**	wide
brutto	ugly	**lungo**	long
buono	good	**piccolo**	small
cattivo	bad	**vecchio**	old

| **è una bella donna** | **il brutto anatroccolo** |
| she is a beautiful woman | the ugly duckling |

But a change in position can affect the force of the adjective. The adjective is given more emphasis if it is placed after the noun:

una vecchia automobile	**un'automobile vecchia**
an old car	an *old* car
è una vecchia automobile	**è un'automobile brutta e vecchia**
it's an old car	it's an awful old car

Sometimes positioning an adjective in front of a noun can have the effect of drawing attention away from it as the main emphatic word in a description:

una proposta intelligente
an intelligent proposal

l'intelligente proposta del ministro
the minister's intelligent proposal

3. Certain adjectives should always follow the noun:

a) Adjectives indicating colour, shape, nationality and religion, and past participles used as adjectives:

la bandiera rossa	**il papa polacco**
the red flag	the Polish pope
la tavola rotonda	**la chiesa cattolica**
the round table	the Catholic Church
la biancheria pulita	**un panino mezzo mangiato**
(the) clean linen	a half-eaten roll

b) Adjectives which are modified by an adverb:

una giornata abbastanza calda
a rather hot day

4. Certain adjectives change their meaning according to their position. As a general rule when they follow the noun their meaning is literal, when they precede the noun a more figurative, abstract meaning is conveyed. Certain adjectives completely change their meaning according to their position:

	BEFORE NOUN	AFTER NOUN
buono	good	(morally) good
caro	dear	expensive
certo	some, certain	sure, reliable
diverso	several (*diversi*)	different
grande	great	big, tall, large
vario	several (*varii*)	different

nuovo	another	new
povero	unfortunate	poor, without money
semplice	just, only	simple, naive
solo	single, only	alone, lonely
unico	single	unique
vero	real	true

un buon amico	**un amico buono**
a good friend	a good-hearted friend
un pover' uomo	**un uomo povero**
an unfortunate man	a man without money
certi risultati	**risultati certi**
certain results	reliable results
diverse persone	**teorie diverse**
several people	different theories
una grande opera	**una camicia grande**
a great work	a large shirt
un nuovo vestito	**un'automobile nuova**
another dress	a (brand) new car
un semplice ragazzo	**un ragazzo semplice**
just a boy	a naive boy
un vero attaccabrighe	**una storia vera**
a real troublemaker	a true story

5. In Italian, unlike English, it is possible to place one adjective before and one after the same noun:

> **un famoso calciatore italiano**
> a famous Italian footballer

F.   COMPARATIVE AND SUPERLATIVE OF ADJECTIVES

Persons or things can be compared by using:

1. *the comparative form of the adjective:*
   more ... than, ...-er than, less ... than, as ... as
2. *the relative superlative form of the adjective:*
   the most ..., the ...-est, the least ...
3. *the absolute superlative form of the adjective:*
   very ...

1. Comparative

The comparative is formed as follows:

a) **più... (di/che)**
more ... / ...-er (than)

più contento   **più caro**
happier   more expensive

Maria è più alta di Nadia
Maria is taller than Nadia

mio padre è più vecchio di mia madre
my father is older than my mother

b) **meno ... (di/che)**
less ... (than)

meno intelligente   **meno reale**
less intelligent   less real

Paola è meno attraente di te
Paola is less attractive than you

Note: in comparatives type **a)** and **b)** **di** is usually used for 'than' before numerals, pronouns and nouns, while **che** is usually used for 'than' before adjectives, adverbs, prepositions, participles and infinitives:

Paola è più ricca di Giorgio
Paola is richer than Giorgio

la mia moto è costata più della tua
my motorbike cost more than yours

questo giardino è più lungo che largo
this garden is longer than it is wide

questo è un libro più divertente che istruttivo
this book is more amusing than instructive

c) **(tanto) ... quanto**   as ... as
(così) ... come

il calcio è tanto popolare in Gran Bretagna quanto in Italia
football is as popular in Great Britain as it is in Italy

Note: the two forms **quanto** and **come** are often interchangeable. With both, the first term is frequently omitted:

è stanca quanto me/è stanca come me
she is as tired as I am

2.   Relative superlative

The relative superlative indicates that a quality is possessed in the highest degree in relation to a group of people or things. It is formed by adding the appropriate definite article to the comparative:

il/la/i/le più ... (di)
the most ..., the ...-est (of/in)

il/la/i/le meno ... (di)
the least ... (of/in)

il più veloce	**i più intelligenti**
the fastest	the most intelligent

la più giovane della famiglia
the youngest of the family

il corridore più veloce del mondo
the fastest runner in the world

le persone meno attive del reparto
the least active people in the department

Note:
i)   when a superlative adjective follows a noun which is preceded by the definite article, the article is not repeated:

l'animale più fedele	**i bambini più viziati**
the most faithful animal	the most spoilt children

ii)   'in' is usually translated by **di**:

la ragazza più carina della scuola
the prettiest girl in the school

Cortina è la località più celebre delle Dolomiti
Cortina is the most famous resort in the Dolomites

iii)   when a possessive adjective is used, the definite article precedes the possessive and is not repeated before **più**:

il suo bisogno più immediato
his/her most immediate need

3.   Absolute superlative

The absolute superlative indicates that a quality is possessed in a very high degree with no relation to other people or things. It could be formed:

a) By adding **-issimo/a/i/e** to the adjective after dropping the final vowel:

vecchio	**vecchissimo**
old	very old
utile	**utilissimo**
useful	very useful
bella	**bellissima**
beautiful	very beautiful
veloci	**velocissimi**
quick	very quick
piccole	**piccolissime**
small	very small
un carissimo amico	**una grammatica utilissima**
a very dear friend	a very useful grammar

Note:

i) adjectives ending in **-co** and **-go** with the plural in **-chi** and **-ghi** drop their final vowel and add an **h** before **-issimo/a/i/e**:

antico
un vaso antichissimo　　a very ancient vase

ii) adjectives ending in **-co** and **-go** with the plural in **-ci** and **-gi** simply drop their final vowel before **-issimo/a/i/e**:

pratico
una borsa praticissima　　a very handy bag

iii) adjectives ending in **-io** which drop the final **-i** in the plural, drop both final vowels before **-issimo/a/i/e**:

vecchio
degli stivali vecchissimi　　some very old boots

Note: not all adjectives can have this form

b) By placing **molto, assai** before the adjective:

assai bella	**molto ubriaco**
very beautiful	very drunk

c) Alternative forms:

i) by using another adjective to strengthen the meaning of the first adjective:

sono stanca *morta*
I'm dead tired

ii) by placing **arci-, stra-, ultra-** before the adjective:

è *stra*ricco
he's very rich

iii) by repeating the adjective:

se ne stava seduto buono buono in un angolo
he was sitting very quietly in a corner

4. Irregular comparatives and superlatives

Some Italian adjectives have irregular as well as regular forms:

ADJ	COMP	RELATIVE SUPERL	ABSOLUTE SUPERL
buono good	**migliore** better	**il migliore** the best	**ottimo** excellent
cattivo bad	**peggiore** worse	**il peggiore** the worst	**pessimo** very bad
grande great	**maggiore** greater, elder	**il maggiore** the greatest, the eldest	**massimo** very great
piccolo small	**minore** smaller, younger, lesser	**il minore** the smallest, the youngest, the least	**minimo** very small, minute

Note:

i) regular and irregular forms are usually interchangeable:

è il migliore caffè che abbia mai bevuto
è il più buon caffè che abbia mai bevuto
it's the best coffee I've ever had

ii) the forms **maggiore, minore** are normally used for age. In other contexts they usually mean 'greater/lesser in importance', while **più grande, più piccolo** mean 'greater/lesser in size':

la tua sorella maggiore   il male minore
your elder sister   the lesser evil

l'appartamento più piccolo
the smaller flat

G. SUFFIXES

As with nouns, the meaning of some adjectives can be altered through the addition of suffixes (different endings):

a) The suffixes **-ino/a**, **-etto/a**, **-ello/a**, **-ellino/a** are generally diminutives:

cattivo bad, naughty	**cattivello** rather bad, naughty
piccola small	**piccolina** rather small

b) The suffixes **-one/a** increase the idea of size expressed by the adjective or strengthen its meaning:

simpatico nice, pleasant	**simpaticone** rather/very nice

c) The suffixes **-astro/a** and **-accio/a** give the adjective a pejorative connotation:

ricco rich	**riccastro** stinking rich
rosso	**ha degli strani capelli rossastri** he/she has strange reddish hair

5. ADVERBS

An adverb is an invariable part of speech which, when used in conjunction with a verb, an adjective, or another adverb, modifies and enriches its meaning. The main categories of adverb are those of Manner, Time, Place, Quantity and Intensity, Affirmation, Negation and Doubt.

A. ADVERBS OF MANNER

These answer the question 'How?' and constitute the largest category.

1. They are commonly formed by adding **-mente** to the adjective (the equivalent of '-ly' in English):

a) If the adjective ends in **-o**, **-mente** is added to the feminine form:

ADJECTIVE		ADVERB
MASC	FEM	
vero (true)	**vera** (true)	**veramente** (really, truly)
esatto	**esatta** (exact)	**esattamente** (exactly)
lento	**lenta** (slow)	**lentamente** (slowly)
affettuoso	**affettuosa** (affectionate)	**affettuosamente** (affectionately)

But: the following are exceptions to the rules given above:

ADJECTIVE	ADVERB
violento (violent)	**violentemente** (violently)
fraudolento (fraudulent)	**fraudolentemente** (fraudulently)
benevolo (benevolent)	**benevolmente** (benevolently)
malevolo (malevolent)	**malevolmente** (malevolently)
leggero (light)	**leggermente** (lightly)

b) If the adjective ends in **-e**, the adverb is formed by simply adding **-mente**:

ADJECTIVE	ADVERB
dolce (sweet)	**dolcemente** (sweetly)
cortese (polite)	**cortesemente** (politely)
veloce (swift)	**velocemente** (swiftly)

c) With adjectives ending in **-le** and **-re** preceded by a vowel, the final **-e** is dropped:

ADJECTIVE	ADVERB
speciale (special)	**specialmente** (specially)
gentile (nice, kind)	**gentilmente** (nicely, kindly)
particolare (particular)	**particolarmente** (particularly)
regolare (regular)	**regolarmente** (regularly)

Note: where **-le** and **-re** are preceded by a consonant, formation of the adverb is regular, for example:

acre (bitter) **acremente** (bitterly)

2. Some very common adverbs are completely irregular:

ADJECTIVE	ADVERB
buono (good)	**bene** (well)
cattivo (bad)	**male** (badly)
migliore (better)	**meglio** (better)

3. Some adverbs have no relation to adjectives at all:

adagio (slowly)
volentieri (willingly)
altrimenti (otherwise)

4. A small number of adverbs, for example the following, end in **-oni**:

bocconi	flat on one's face
carponi	on all fours
ginocchioni	on one's knees
a tentoni	gropingly
a cavalcioni	astride

5. Certain adjectives in their masculine singular form may be used instead of adverbs:

parlare piano	to speak softly
vedere chiaro	to see clearly
lavorare sodo	to work hard
abitare vicino	to live nearby
piovere forte	to rain heavily
tagliare corto	to cut short
stare fermo	to stand still

6. Alternative ways of forming adverbs:

a) An adverb can be replaced by an adverbial phrase, for example **in modo, in maniera** + adjective:

> **agire in un modo strano**
> to act strangely
>
> **rispondere in una maniera sgarbata**
> to reply rudely

b) Preposition + noun:

con calma	calmly
con eleganza	elegantly
senza paura	fearlessly
senza difficoltà	easily
a malincuore	reluctantly
in fretta	hastily

c) Other adverbial phrases (see also p 66):

di buon grado	willingly
ad occhio nudo	with the naked eye

B. ADVERBS OF TIME

These answer the question 'When?'. Here are some common examples:

oggi	today
ieri	yesterday
domani	tomorrow
stamattina	this morning
stasera	this evening
stanotte	last night, tonight
ora, adesso	now
allora, poi	then
subito	immediately, at once
prima	before
dopo	after, afterwards
spesso	often
sempre	always
presto	soon, early, quickly
tardi	late
già	already
ancora	still, yet, again
finora	until now, so far

ormai, oramai	by now, by then, by this time
infine	in the end, finally
intanto	meanwhile
mai	ever, never

| **scrivimi presto** | **mi sono alzato presto** |
| write to me soon | I got up early |

| **muoviamoci, presto!** | **sta ancora mangiando** |
| let's move, quickly! | he/she's still eating |

| **aspetta ancora una settimana** | **non sono ancora pronto** |
| wait another week | I'm not ready yet |

| **non sei mai a casa** | **sei mai stato a Milano?** |
| you are never at home | have you ever been to Milan? |

Note: some adverbs of place like **prima** and **dopo** are also used as prepositions:

me l'ha confessato dopo	**telefonerò dopo le vacanze**
he/she confessed it to me	I'll ring up after my holidays
afterwards (*adverb*)	(*preposition*)

Note: for adverbial phrases of time, see also p 66.

C. ADVERBS OF PLACE

These answer the question 'Where?'. Here are some common examples:

qui, qua	here
lì, là	there
qua e là	here and there
sotto	under, below
sopra	up, on, above
fuori	out, outside
dentro	in, inside
su	on, up
giù	down
quassù	up here
quaggiù	down here
lassù	up there
laggiù	down there
lontano	far away
vicino	near, nearby
dietro	behind
(d)avanti	in front
indietro	behind
intorno	around

dappertutto	everywhere
dovunque	everywhere
altrove	elsewhere
avanti!	**su le mani!**
come in!	hands up!
gli uffici sono sopra	**c'è scritto sopra il mio nome**
the offices are above	my name is written on it
qua sopra ci sono i dizionari	**c'è una farmacia qui vicino**
the dictionaries are up here	there's a chemist near here

Note: some adverbs of place, such as **sopra, sotto, su, dentro, fuori, davanti, dietro, intorno**, etc also function as prepositions:

guarda su!	**il libro è sul tavolo**
look up	the book is on the table
(adverb)	*(preposition)*

Note: adverbial particles **ci** (here, there), **vi** (here, there) and **ne** (from there) are dealt with in the Pronoun section (see pp 76-80).

D.   ADVERBS OF QUANTITY AND INTENSITY

This category answers the question 'To what extent?'or 'With how much intensity?'. Here are some common examples:

quanto*	how much
molto*	a lot, much, very
assai	very
poco*	little
un po'	a little
tanto*	so much
abbastanza	enough
parecchio*	quite a lot
troppo*	too much
così	so
talmente	so
nulla, niente	nothing
appena	hardly, scarcely, just
almeno	at least
alquanto	somewhat
più	more
meno	less
solo, soltanto	only

altrettanto	as much, so much
quasi	almost
sono appena partiti	**posso vederlo appena**
they have just left	I can hardly see him
quanto costa?	**li vedo molto poco**
how much does it cost?	I very seldom see them

Note: the adverbs with an asterisk must not be confused with the corresponding adjectives or pronouns:

ho mangiato molto	**ho mangiato molti biscotti**
I've eaten a lot	I've eaten a lot of biscuits
(*adverb*)	(*adjective*)
ne ho mangiati molti	
I've eaten many of them	
(*pronoun*)	

E. ADVERBS OF AFFIRMATION, NEGATION AND DOUBT

1. Affirmation

sì	yes
certo, certamente	certainly
sicuro, sicuramente	certainly, surely
senz'altro	certainly
senza dubbio	undoubtedly
veramente	really, truly
davvero	really, truly
appunto	precisely

hai fame? - sì	**vi piace la musica? - sì**
are you hungry? - yes, I am	do you like music? - yes, we do
ti piace davvero?	
do you really like it?	

2. Negation

no	no
non	not
nemmeno	not even
mai	never
niente, nulla	nothing
non...affatto	not ... at all
giammai	never

è vero? - no
is it true? - no, it's not

hai letto questo libro? - no
have you read this book? - no, I haven't

no, non ci credo!
no, I don't believe it!

non ci sono mai stato
I've never been there

non gli ho nemmeno parlato
I didn't even speak to him

non ho affatto fame
I'm not in the least hungry

sei stanco? - niente affatto
are you tired? - not at all

Note: for further treatment of negative expressions see pp 233-7

3. Doubt

forse	perhaps, maybe
probabilmente	probably
quasi	almost
perché	why
eventualmente	if necessary, if need be

eventualmente verrò domani
if necessary, I'll come tomorrow

F. COMPARATIVE AND SUPERLATIVE OF ADVERBS

1. For adverbs of manner (except the ones ending in **-oni**), and a few adverbs of time and place, the formation of the comparative and superlative parallels that of adjectives. The superlative is formed by adding **-issimo** to the stem of the adverb; if the adverb ends with **-mente**, then **-issima** + **-mente** are added:

ADVERB	COMPARATIVE	SUPERLATIVE
lentamente slowly	**più lentamente** more slowly	**lentissimamente** very slowly
spesso often	**più spesso** more often	**spessissimo** very often
lontano far	**più lontano** further	**lontanissimo** very far

ha reagito più rapidamente del solito
he/she has reacted more swiftly than usual

oggi finiremo più tardi di ieri
today we'll finish later than yesterday

2. Irregular comparatives and superlatives

ADVERB	COMPARATIVE	SUPERLATIVE
bene well	**meglio** better	**ottimamente/benissimo** very well
male badly	**peggio** worse	**pessimamente/malissimo** very badly
molto much, very	**più** more	**moltissimo** very much
poco little	**meno** less	**pochissimo** very little
grandemente greatly	**maggiormente** more	**massimamente** most, mostly

3. Use

a) Contrast between English and Italian use of the superlative

As seen in the above tables the Italian adverbial superlative is normally used to express the idea of 'very ...'

Whereas it is common in English to form constructions of the type 'he trained the hardest' or 'this printer prints the fastest', Italian will tend to use a different type of construction to express the same idea:

di tutte le stampanti questa è quella che stampa più velocemente
di tutte le stampanti questa è la più veloce a stampare
of all the printers this one prints the fastest

sicuramente fuma meno di tutti gli altri
rispetto agli altri è quello che fuma meno
compared with the rest he definitely smokes the least

le persone che sono arrivate per prime sono quelle che sono rimaste più a lungo
the people who arrived first also stayed the longest

l'automobile che si è comportata meglio nelle prove
the car which performed (the) best in the trials

b)   The superlative may be expressed in other ways:

   i)   by placing **molto** (very), **assai** (very) or **estremamente** (extremely) in front of the adverb

   guidava la macchina assai lentamente
   he/she drove his/her car very slowly

   ii) in a limited number of cases, by duplication of the adjective or adverb.

pian(o) piano	very slowly, very softly
lento lento	very slowly

c)   Superlative with **il più/meno … possibile** (as … as possible):

   vorrei andare in vacanza il più lontano possibile
   I'd like to go on holiday as far away as possible

   scrivimi il più presto possibile
   write to me as soon as possible

d)   Comparative with **meno** (less):

   ci ha telefonato meno spesso quest'anno
   he/she has phoned us less often this year

G.   ADDITIONAL POINTS

1.   Adverbial Phrases

Commonly used expressions such as the following have an adverbial function:

sempre (di) più	more and more
sempre (di) meno	less and less
sempre più veloce	faster and faster
più o meno	more or less
al più presto	as quickly as possible
di bene in meglio	better and better
di male in peggio	worse and worse
meno male	thank goodness, just as well
meglio/peggio che mai	better/worse than ever
tanto meglio/peggio	so much the better/worse
alla meglio	as best one can
di tanto in tanto	every so often
ogni tanto	every so often
d'ora in poi	from now on
a poco a poco	little by little

di buon'ora	early
ad un tratto	suddenly
all'improvviso	unexpectedly
all'italiana	Italian-style

2. Suffixes

In rare cases adverbs may be modified by suffixes:

bene	well
benino	tolerably well
benone	extremely well
male	badly
maluccio	not too well
poco	little
pochino	rather little
ho mangiato poco	**ho mangiato pochino**
I ate little	I ate rather little

3. Position of Adverbs

a) Although the position of adverbs may sometimes be varied for reasons of emphasis or expressiveness, they normally follow the verb they modify:

ci ha salutato molto gentilmente
he/she greeted us very kindly

abito lontano
I live far away

Note, however, the position of the following common adverbs of time when the verb is in a compound tense:

te l'ho *già* detto mille volte
I have already told you a thousand times

non ho *mai* visto una cosa simile!
I've never seen such a thing!

b) When the adverb modifies an adjective or another adverb it usually precedes it:

sono arrivato molto tardi
I arrived very late

il suo comportamento è stato poco dignitoso
his/her behaviour was not very dignified

6. PRONOUNS

PERSONAL PRONOUNS

There are four categories of personal pronouns:
- **subject** pronouns
- **object** pronouns
- **disjunctive** pronouns
- **reflexive** pronouns

For reflexive pronouns see p 115.

A. SUBJECT PRONOUNS

1. Forms

PERSON	SINGULAR		PLURAL	
1st	**io**	I	**noi**	we
2nd	**tu**	you	**voi**	you
3rd	**lui (egli, esso)**	he, it	**loro (essi)**	they (*masc*)
	lei (ella, essa)	she, it	**loro (esse)**	they (*fem*)
polite				
forms	**lei**	you	**loro**	you

2. Use

a) **tu** and **voi** are the singular and plural forms used when speaking to relatives, friends, children and animals.

b) **lui**, **lei** and **loro** are now the most commonly used third person pronouns, particularly in spoken Italian. The forms **egli** and **ella**, as well as **essi** and **esse**, are now mainly found in the written language. **esso** and **essa** are used to refer to animals, inanimate objects or abstractions, but are frequently omitted.

c) Polite forms are used when speaking to an older or unknown person:

i) **lei** is the singular polite form of address. **loro** is the plural, although there is a growing tendency, particularly in the spoken language, to replace the latter with the **voi** form.

lei and loro may be written with initial capitals (**Lei, Loro**) particularly in formal letters.

lei and loro *always* take the *third* person singular and plural forms of the verb respectively:

lei è veramente fortunato/a!
you're really lucky!

studiano loro?
are you studying?

ii) **voi** is used as a singular polite form in some regions of Italy and is common in commercial correspondence.

Note: the following expression is particularly associated with the use of the informal second person or formal (polite) third person pronoun forms:

dare del tu   **dare del lei**
to use the 'tu' form   to use the 'lei' form

diamoci del tu
let's use the 'tu' form

d) The subject pronouns may be followed by **stesso** (which agrees with its subject) in order to express 'myself', 'yourself' etc:

io stesso ho parlato con la preside
I myself have spoken to the headmistress

e) Italian uses subject pronouns with the verb 'to be' in the following type of construction:

chi è? - sono io (siamo noi ecc.)
who is it? - it's me (it's us etc)

Also without a verb:

chi? io?
who? me?

3. Omission of pronouns

The subject pronouns are frequently omitted in Italian as the verb endings are often sufficient to indicate the person:

non voglio
I don't want to

che cosa avete detto?
what did you say?

They may be used, however:

a) For clarity (eg with the singular persons of the present subjunctive which have the same form):

  hanno paura che io abbia perso le chiavi
  they are afraid I have lost the keys

b) For emphasis:

  pago io   *I'm* paying
  tu che ne pensi?   what do *you* think of it?
  pensaci tu!   *you* think about it!
  me l'hanno detto loro   *they* told me

c) For contrast:

  io vado in piscina, lui invece rimane a casa
  I'm going to the swimming baths but he's staying at home

d) Subject pronouns must not be omitted after adverbs such as **anche**, **neppure** etc:

  anche voi dovete provare   **vengo anch'io!**
  you must try too   I'm coming too!

  neppure noi abbiamo voglia di vederli
  we don't want to see them either

B. OBJECT PRONOUNS

These are also known as conjunctive pronouns or weak pronouns. They cannot stand by themselves but must be used in conjunction with a verb. Object pronouns include:

  - direct object pronouns
  - indirect object pronouns
  - the particles **ne** and **ci (vi)**

1. Forms

PERSON	DIRECT		INDIRECT	
1st sing	**mi**	me	**mi**	to me
2nd sing	**ti**	you	**ti**	to you
3rd sing	**lo**	him, it	**gli**	to him, to it
	la	her, it	**le**	to her, to it

1st plural	**ci**	us	**ci**	to us
2nd plural	**vi**	you	**vi**	to you
3rd plural	**li**	them (*masc*)	**loro**	to them (*masc*)
	le	them (*fem*)	**loro**	to them (*fem*)

polite forms				
sing	**la**	you (*masc, fem*)	**le**	to you (*masc, fem*)
plural	**li**	you (*masc*)	**loro**	to you (*masc, fem*)
	le	you (*fem*)		

non lo conosco	**vi hanno risposto?**
I don't know him	have they replied to you?

2. Use

a) **lo** is often used in Italian as a neuter pronoun which may be omitted when translating into English:

> **Gigi si è sposato - lo so!**
> Gigi got married - I know!

It may also substitute for an entire phrase in order to avoid repetition:

> **preferite andare in treno? - sì, lo preferiamo**
> do you prefer going by train? - yes, we do

b) In spoken Italian **gli** is tending to replace **loro** to mean 'to them' (of course it can also mean 'to him'):

> **gli ho detto di sbrigarsi**
> I told him/them to hurry up

c) Elision of pronouns is common with third person singular direct object pronouns in the perfect and pluperfect tenses but may also occur with the first and second persons singular; these latter also tend to elide when followed by a verb beginning with **i**:

> **m'hanno fatto ridere tanto**
> they made me laugh such a lot

> **t'interessa vedere di nuovo quel film?**
> are you interested in seeing that film again?

> **l'ho visto due volte**
> I saw him twice

> **l'abbiamo invitata all'ultimo momento**
> we invited her at the last minute

But with third person plural direct object pronouns there is no elision:

li ho visti due volte
I saw them twice

le abbiamo invitate all'ultimo momento
we invited them at the last minute

d) Certain verbs requiring a direct object in English, must be followed by an indirect object in Italian:

le telefoneremo
we'll ring her up

credigli!
believe him/them!

Certain verbs requiring the indirect object in English, must be followed by a direct object in Italian:

ascoltami
listen to me

l'aspetterò all'angolo
I'll wait for him/her at the corner

Particular care must be taken in Italian with verbs which also require an indirect pronoun in English, although the fact that one pronoun *is* an indirect pronoun may not be obvious:

gli ho mandato un assegno
I sent him/them a cheque = I sent a cheque to him/them

This would also be the case with the following verbs:

comprare to buy	**vendere** to sell
mostrare to show	**prestare** to lend
dare to give	**offrire** to offer
dire to tell	

le ho comprato un paio di scarpe
I bought her a pair of shoes

prestagli mille lire
lend him/them a thousand lire

3. Agreement

In compound tenses, the participle always agrees with the preceding third person direct object pronoun:

hai già scritto la lettera? - sì, l'ho scritta ieri
have you written the letter already? - yes, I wrote it yesterday

avete chiesto le informazioni? - sì, le abbiamo già chieste
have you asked for the information? - yes, we have already asked
for it

Agreement is optional in the case of the first and second person:

ti ho visto in centro ieri, Silvia
ti ho vista in centro ieri, Silvia
I saw you in town yesterday, Silvia

non ci hanno visto
non ci hanno visti/e
they didn't see us

4.   Position

a)   All object pronouns precede a finite verb (the auxiliary in the case of
compound tenses) EXCEPT the third person plural indirect object
pronoun **loro** ('to them', 'to you' *polite*):

gli **ho dato uno schiaffo**
I gave him a slap

non *ci* **hanno mai incoraggiati**
they have never encouraged us

avevo dato *loro* **il mio numero di telefono**
I had given them my phone number

Note: the negative **non** precedes the pronouns.

b)   In the cases outlined below, however, the object pronouns are
added to the end of the verb form:

i)   with infinitives, in which case the final **e** is dropped:

sono venuto per aiutar*ti*
I've come to help you

va' a dir*gli* la buona notizia
go and tell him/them the good news

ha continuato a guardar*la*
he went on looking at her

ii)   with modal verbs plus an infinitive there are two possibilities:

non voglio veder*lo* più
non *lo* voglio più vedere
I don't want to see him any more

posso far*le* una domanda?
or   ***le* posso fare una domanda?**
may I ask you a question?

  iii) with gerunds:

     ***lo* stava osservando**
     stava osservando*lo*
     he/she was observing him/it

     osservando*lo* attentamente
     observing him/it closely

     avendo*li* comprati, adesso vogliamo vender*li* al più presto
     having bought them, we now want to sell them as soon as possible

  iv) with past participles standing alone:

     finito*lo*   having finished it
     parlato*gli*   having spoken to him

  v) with informal imperatives:

     perdona*mi*   forgive me
     scrivete*lo*   write it
     ascoltiamo*li*   let's listen to them
     dim*mi*   tell me
     fa*lo* subito   do it right away

     For the position of pronouns with both formal and informal imperatives, and for the doubling of consonants in the last two examples above, see also p 146.

Note: with the negative imperative two pronoun positions are possible:

     non legger*lo*
or   **non *lo* leggere**
     don't read it

  vi) with ecco:

     ecco*lo*! here he (it) is!   **ecco*ci*!** here we are!
     ecco*mi*! here I am!   **ecco*li*!** here they are!

Note: in all these above cases the third person plural indirect pronoun **loro** follows the verb and remains separate from it:

     ho voluto vendere loro la casa
     I wanted to sell them the house

     avendo insegnato loro come si pronuncia questa parola...
     having taught them how this word is pronounced ...

parla loro
speak to them

5. Order of object pronouns

When direct and indirect pronouns are used together, the indirect precedes the direct and the following changes occur: the indirect object pronouns **mi, ti, ci, vi** and the third person reflexive pronoun **si** become **me, te, ce, ve** and **se**:

me lo	me la	me li	me le
te lo	te la	te li	te le
se lo	se la	se li	se le
ce lo	ce la	ce li	ce le
ve lo	ve la	ve li	ve le
se lo	se la	se li	se le

me lo presterai?   **me l'ha detto**
will you lend it to me?   he/she told me

ce li hanno presentati
they introduced them to us

se lo ripete spesso
he often repeats it to himself

gli and **le** (also in the polite form) become **glie-** and combine with the direct object pronoun to give:

glielo, gliela, glieli and **gliele**

Note: **glielo/a/i/e** can have a range of meanings:

glielo manderò
I'll send it to him/her/them (*masc* or *fem*)/you (*polite form, sing* or *plur, masc* or *fem*).

gliel'ho sempre detto
I have always told him/her/them/you that

glieli abbiamo già inviati
we have already sent them to him/her/them/you

vorrei regalarglielo
I would like to give it to him/her/them/you as a present

For the position of object pronouns, and in particular of **loro**, see also pp 73-5.

C. THE PARTICLE *NE*

Ne (and also **ci** (**vi**)) has both an adverbial and a pronominal function. In neither case, however, can the particle stand by itself. Instead it must be used in conjunction with a verb in the same way as object pronouns.

In its pronominal function **ne** has a range of meanings including 'of it/him/her/them', 'about it/him/her/them', 'of this/that', 'some' and 'any'.

1. Use

a)   It is particularly associated with the preposition **di**:

   i)   to replace **di** + noun or pronoun:

   che cosa sai *di quest'affare*? - non *ne* so nulla
   what do you know about this affair? - I don't know anything
   about it

   avete bisogno *della macchina* stasera? - no, non *ne* abbiamo bisogno
   do you need the car this evening? - no, we don't need it

   cosa pensi *di Gianni*? - che *ne* pensi?
   what do you think of Gianni? - what do you think of him?

   non me *ne* importa niente
   I couldn't care less about it

   ii)   to replace some clauses introduced by **di**. Many Italian verbs can
   be followed by the preposition **di**, for example: **dimenticarsi** (to
   forget), **rallegrarsi** (to be pleased), **accorgersi** (to notice), **rendersi
   conto** (to realize), **pentirsi** (to regret), **servirsi** (to use) etc, see also
   pp 190-1:

   **mi sono dimenticato *di dar da mangiare al gatto* - me *ne* sono
   dimenticato**
   I forgot to feed the cat - I forgot about it

   quella ragazza ha agito da sciocca, ma adesso se *ne* pente
   that girl acted like an idiot, but now she regrets it

b)   To replace the partitive (**del, della, dei** etc):

   hai comprato *dei libri di Calvino*? - no, non *ne* ho comprati
   did you buy any books by Calvino? - no, I didn't buy any

   c'è ancora *del denaro da spendere*? - no, non ce *n'*è più
   is there some money left to spend? - no, there isn't any left

c)   **ne** is essential with numerals and adjectives of quantity when the
   noun is not repeated and a verb is used. It should be noted that

whereas in the following Italian examples **ne** is essential, it will not usually be translated into English:

quanti *anni* hai? - *ne* ho diciassette
how old are you? - I'm seventeen

che belle *pesche*! *ne* comprerò un chilo
what wonderful peaches! I'll buy a kilo

come mi piacciono questi *cioccolatini*! *ne* ho mangiati tantissimi!
how I love these chocolates! I've eaten ever so many of them!

d)   in its adverbial function **ne** means 'from there/here' and is associated with the preposition **da**:

è facile entrare nel labirinto - il difficile è uscir*ne*
it is easy to get into the maze - the difficulty lies in getting out of it

vatte*ne*!
go away!

2.   Position

a)   **ne** precedes the verb except in the cases described on pp 73-5:

ne **hai parlato col padrone? - no, non *ne* ho ancora parlato con lui**
have you spoken to the boss about it? - no, I haven't spoken to him about it yet

b)   Where it is used in conjunction with an indirect object pronoun or a reflexive pronoun it takes second place:

te *ne* parlerò domani
I'll speak to you about it tomorrow

non me *ne* intendo molto
I don't know much about it

me *ne* andrò domani
I'm going away tomorrow

vorrei andarme*ne*
I'd like to go away

parliamoglie*ne*, se vuoi
let's talk to him/her/them about it, if you want

posso parlarve*ne* un attimo?
may I speak to you about it for a moment?

Note: **ecco*ne* due!**
here are two of them!

3. Agreement

ne can agree with the past participle only in its partitive use (see also p 158):

ho bevuto *della birra* - *ne* hai bevuta anche tu?
I have had some beer - have you had some too?

D. THE PARTICLE *CI (VI)*

ci and vi are object pronouns, but they can also be used as adverbs. vi is identical to ci but is used rather less, particularly in spoken Italian. The choice between the two is usually made on phonetic or stylistic grounds, for instance, in order to avoid alliteration in a phrase such as **vi vado** (I'm going there), the form **ci vado** is preferred.

In their pronominal function ci (vi) could have a range of different meanings including 'to it/them/this/that', 'of it/them/this/that', 'about it/them/this/that', 'on it/them/this/that', etc.

1. Use

a) They are particularly associated with the preposition a 'to':

i)   to replace **a** + noun or pronoun:

crede *alle promesse* fatte dalle autorità? - no, non *ci* credo
do you believe in the promises made by the authorities? - no, I don't believe in them

pensi *all'avvenire*? - sì, *ci* penso spesso
do you think about the future? - yes, I often think about it

ii) to replace **a** + verb:

sei riuscito *a portare quella valigia alla stazione*? - no, non *ci* sono riuscito, ho dovuto prendere un taxi
did you manage to carry that suitcase to the station? - no, I didn't; I had to get a taxi

provate *a spiegarglielo più chiaramente* - *ci* proveremo!
try to explain it to him more clearly - we'll try to

iii) to replace other constructions:

egli crede *che Paolo sia snob*, ma io non *ci* credo
he thinks that Paolo is a snob, but I don't think so

mi dispiace, non so che farci!
I'm sorry, I don't know what to do about it!

ci penseremo domani
we'll think about it tomorrow

ci puoi contare
you can depend on it

ci puoi scommettere!
you can bet on it!

b) In their adverbial function **ci (vi)** mean 'there' and 'to there' and are associated principally with the preposition **a** but also with **in** and **su**:

sei mai stato *a Pisa*? - sì, *ci* sono stato diverse volte
have you ever been to Pisa? - yes, I have been there a number of times

***ci* siamo rimasti due mesi**
we stayed there for two months

a che ora vai *a scuola*? - *ci* vado alle otto e mezzo
at what time do you go to school? - I go at half past eight

ti piacerebbe vivere *in Italia*? - sì, mi piacerebbe viver*ci*
would you like to live in Italy? - yes, I would like to live there

2. Position

Like **ne** and the other object pronouns, **ci (vi)** precede the verb except in the cases described in section B4b) above:

***ci* andrò domani**
I'll go there tomorrow

***ci* è già stata altre volte**
she has already been there on other occasions

andiamo*ci* stasera
let's go there this evening

In combination with other pronouns, **ci (vi)** precede **lo, la, li, le** and **ne** and change their form to **ce (ve)**:

***ce* l'ho messo io!**
I put it there

mi dispiace, non *ce* ne sono più
I'm sorry, there aren't any left

But: **ci (vi)** follow **mi** and **ti**:

mi *ci* troverai ogni sabato sera
you will find me there every Saturday evening

Note: alternative modes of expression, such as the adverbs of place **lì** or **là**, may be substituted.

3. With reflexives

When using **ci (vi)** with a reflexive verb their relation to the reflexive pronoun varies as follows:

> mi *CI* abituo (I'm getting used to it)
> ti *CI* abitui (you're getting used to it)
> *CI* si abitua (one/he/she's/you're getting used to it)
> *VI* ci abituiamo (we're getting used to it)*
> vi *CI* abituate (you're getting used to it)
> *CI* si abituano (they're/you're getting used to it)

* vi is used here to avoid the repetitive **ci ci** (although this is rare)

Note: the following uses of **ci (vi)**:

> hai *il passaporto*? - sì, *ce* l'ho
> have you got a passport? - yes, I have

> avete *cinquemila lire*, per caso? - ci dispiace, non *ce* le abbiamo
> have you got five thousand lire by any chance? - no, sorry, we haven't

> quanto tempo ci vuole *per andare a Trieste in macchina*? - ci vogliono due ore
> how long does it take to go to Trieste by car? - it takes two hours

E.   DISJUNCTIVE PRONOUNS

Unlike the conjunctive pronouns studied above, disjunctive pronouns are not so strongly linked to the verb. They are particularly associated with prepositions.

1.   Forms

PERSON	SINGULAR		PLURAL	
1st	**me**	me	**noi**	us
2nd	**te**	you	**voi**	you
3rd	**lui**	him	**loro**	them (*masc*)
	lei	her	**loro**	them (*fem*)
	esso/a	it	**essi/e**	them
	sé	him/herself	**sé**	themselves
		yourself		yourselves
		itself		
polite forms	**lei**	you	**loro**	you

> vieni con noi   tocca a te
> come with us   it's your turn

Note: for use of the formal and informal pronoun forms, see subject
pronouns p 68

2. Use

a)   When the verb has two direct or indirect objects or one pronoun
and one noun, the disjunctive pronouns must be used in place of
conjunctive pronouns:

> **ho invitato lui ma non lei**
> I invited him but not her

> **hanno fornito le informazioni necessarie a noi ma non a loro**
> they provided us with the necessary information but not them

> **sono piaciuti enormemente a me e a mia sorella**
> my sister and I liked them enormously

b)   For emphasis in place of a conjunctive pronoun:

compare: **non mi hanno detto niente**
> they haven't told me anything

> **a me non hanno detto niente**
> they haven't told *me* anything

and   **non mi sembra brutto**
> it doesn't seem ugly to me

> **a me non sembra brutto**
> it doesn't seem ugly to *me*

c)   With prepositions, including prepositions following verbs:

> **andiamo con loro**   **secondo noi, lui ha torto**
> let's go with them   in our opinion he's wrong

> **è venuta da me ieri sera**   **fra me e te**
> she came to my house   between you and me
> yesterday evening

> **sono venuti incontro a noi**
> they came to meet us

> **pensa solo a sé**
> he/she thinks only of himself/herself

> **dipende da lei**
> it depends on her/you

d)   With comparisons:

> **tu sei più simpatica di lui**
> you are nicer than him

lui è meno esigente di noi
he's less demanding than us

loro sono così (tanto) bravi come (quanto) voi
they're as good as you

e)   With expressions of the following type:

povero me   **beata te**
poor me   lucky you

F.   THE IMPERSONAL PRONOUN *SI*

As an impersonal pronoun, **si** is the equivalent of the English 'one' (or more commonly 'we' or 'they' or 'people'). It is followed by the third person singular of the verb. It has, however, a number of special features which merit close study. In the examples which follow, **si** will be used only with intransitive verbs (or with verbs used intransitively); for its passive function with transitive verbs, see p 163.

a)   At its simplest **si** operates like a subject pronoun:

non si sa mai
one never knows/you never know

ogni giorno si lavora dalle nove alle cinque
every day we work from nine till five

di solito si mangia all'una
we normally eat at one o'clock

si va via?
shall we leave?

b)   When followed by the verbs **essere, restare, rimanere, stare** and **diventare**, **si** requires a plural adjective:

quando si è giovani, non si accetta sempre di essere criticati
when one is young, one cannot always accept criticism

si rimane sempre soddisfatti di un lavoro ben fatto
one is always satisfied by a job well done

c)   With reflexive verbs **si** changes to **ci** in order to avoid repetition:

durante la settimana ci si alza di buon'ora
during the week we/you get up early

non ci si rende sempre conto del pericolo
one does not always realize the danger

d) In compound tenses when using **si** *all* verbs must be conjugated with **essere** including those which normally take **avere**. Verbs normally conjugated with **essere** will have a plural past participle:

si è studiato tutta la settimana
we've been studying all week

si è arrivati a Siena alle sette di sera
we arrived in Siena at seven in the evening

non si è capito cosa voleva
we didn't understand what he/she wanted

ci si è abituati al nuovo orario
we got used to the new timetable

e) The position of the pronouns with **si** is as follows: all pronouns precede **si** except **ne** which follows. In the latter case **si** changes to **se**:

lo si dice un po' dappertutto
people are saying it just about everywhere

ci si può andare a piedi
you can go there on foot

se ne discute ogni tanto
we/they discuss it every so often

Note: **si** may be replaced by the indefinite pronoun **uno** which does not have the special features of the former but which is also less frequently used in Italian:

uno si trova bene in questa pensione
one is quite comfortable in this guesthouse

G. POSSESSIVE ADJECTIVES AND PRONOUNS

1. Forms

The forms of possessive adjectives and pronouns are identical in Italian. They are always accompanied by the definite article except in certain clearly defined cases shown below. They agree in number and gender with the object or the person 'possessed':

| SINGULAR | | PLURAL | | |
MASC	FEM	MASC	FEM	
il mio	la mia	i miei	le mie	my, mine
il tuo	la tua	i tuoi	le tue	your, yours
il suo	la sua	i suoi	le sue	his, her, hers, its
il nostro	la nostra	i nostri	le nostre	our, ours
il vostro	la vostra	i vostri	le vostre	your, yours
il loro	la loro	i loro	le loro	their, theirs

polite forms

il suo	la sua	i suoi	le sue	your, yours (*sing*)
il loro	la loro	i loro	le loro	your, yours (*plural*)

il mio cane	**la sua cassetta**
my dog	his/her/your cassette
i suoi vestiti	**le tue impressioni**
his/her/your clothes	your impressions
il suo conto, signore	**i loro affari**
your bill, Sir	their/your business

Note:

i) the possessive forms associated with the polite forms of address are, like the latter, sometimes written with an initial capital letter:

il Suo conto, signore
your bill, Sir

ii) **loro** is invariable (ie it does not change its ending):

la loro automobile	**i loro amici**
their/your car	their/your friends

iii) as the pronoun **voi** may be used as a plural polite form instead of **loro**, so the possessive **il vostro** can also have a polite usage

2. Use of the possessive adjective

a) The possessive adjective is repeated before each noun and agrees with it:

i tuoi blue-jeans e le tue scarpe sono bagnati
your jeans and your shoes are soaking wet

b) Where ambiguities arise concerning the third person possessives, alternative forms may be employed:

la sua giacca
his/her/your jacket

may be expressed more clearly by using the disjunctive pronouns (see p 81). For example:

la giacca di lui
his jacket

la giacca di lei
her/your jacket

or the adjective **proprio** may be used:

Mario andò via con Paolo e prese la propria automobile
Mario left with Paolo and took his own car

c) In Italian, as in French, the possessive adjective itself is often omitted in cases where the identity of the possessor is already clear from the context:

metti il cappotto
put your coat on

hanno chinato la testa
they bent their heads

hai gli occhi più grandi della bocca
your eyes are bigger than your stomach

d) Omission of the definite article with the possessive:

i) with family relationships in the singular, with all possessive adjectives except **loro**:

mia sorella	**nostro cugino**
my sister	our cousin

But: **il loro genero**
their/your son-in-law

In the plural, however, the article is not omitted:

le mie sorelle	**i tuoi cugini**
my sisters	your cousins

Note: the forms **babbo** (dad), **mamma** (mum), **nonno** (grandfather) and **nonna** (grandmother) may be found with or without the definite article (**mio babbo** or **il mio babbo**)

But: if the possessive is used with another adjective or if the noun has a suffix, then the definite article is not omitted:

il tuo fratellino
your little brother

il nostro vecchio padre
our old father

la mia sorella sposata
my married sister

ii)   with certain prepositional phrases:

a mio parere
in my opinion

a vostra disposizione
at your disposal

iii)   when the adjective is placed after the noun:

★   with the vocative case:

Dio mio!
my God!

★   with certain set phrases:

non sono affari vostri
it's none of your business

è colpa mia
it's my fault

casa mia
my house

fa sempre tutto di testa sua
he/she does everything as he/she pleases

e)   Instead of the definite article other parts of speech may be found in conjunction with the possessive adjective:

una mia amica
a friend of mine

due miei amici
two friends of mine

molti miei coetanei
many of my age-group

quel mio collega
that colleague of mine

3.   Use of the possessive pronoun

In the following examples possessive adjectives are used in the first part of the sentence, and possessive pronouns in the second part. The latter simply substitute for the missing noun:

ho dimenticato il mio dizionario; prestami il tuo!
I've forgotten my dictionary - lend me yours!

mia sorella si è laureata l'anno scorso, e la tua?
my sister graduated last year, what about yours?

è carina la tua gonna, mi piace più della mia
your skirt is really nice – I like it better than mine

la loro macchina somiglia molto alla nostra
their/your car looks a lot like ours

Note:

i)   the article is sometimes omitted when the pronoun is preceded by
     essere but there is a slight difference in meaning:

     questa borsa è la mia
     this is my bag (*one of a number*)

     questa borsa è mia
     this is my bag (*my property*)

ii) when a possessive pronoun refers to two preceding nouns of
     different gender the masculine form predominates:

     questa chiave e questo passaporto sono miei
     this key and this passport are mine

H.   INDEFINITE PRONOUNS AND ADJECTIVES

These fall into three categories:

1. Words functioning only as indefinite pronouns
2. Words functioning only as indefinite adjectives
3. Words functioning both as indefinite pronouns and adjectives

1.   Indefinite pronouns

The following cannot be used with a noun and are found only in the
singular:

uno/una	one
ognuno/ognuna	each one, everyone
qualcuno/qualcuna	someone, anyone
qualcosa	something, anything
chiunque	anyone, anything
nulla/niente	nothing

se uno arriva con qualche minuto di ritardo...
if one arrives a minute or two late ...

ognuno deve pensare alle proprie responsabilità
everyone must think about their own responsibilities

qualcuno è venuto a trovarti ma non so chi
somebody came looking for you but I don't know who

vuoi qualcosa da bere?
do you want something to drink?

c'è qualcosa di nuovo?
is there anything new?

chiunque è capace di usare un videoregistratore
anyone can use a video recorder

non ne so niente/nulla di preciso
I don't know anything specific about it

grazie mille! - di niente!
thanks a lot! - don't mention it!

Note:

i)   **uno** does in fact appear in the plural when it is followed by
     altri/e. In this case it is always preceded by the definite article:

     gli uni vogliono andar via, gli altri vogliono restare qui
     some want to go away, (the) others want to stay here

     It has a reciprocal meaning in the phrase **l'un l'altro** used with a
     reflexive verb:

     si battono l'un l'altro
     they're hitting one another

But: with other verbs a preposition must be added:

     discutevano l'uno con l'altro
     they were arguing with one another

ii) **niente,** when it follows the verb, requires a double negation (see
     also p 235):

     non è successo niente
     nothing happened

But: **niente lo fermerà**
     nothing will stop him

2. Indefinite adjectives

These must accompany a noun. All five are invariable.

ogni	each, every
qualche	some, a few
qualsiasi	any, any at all, some ... or other
qualunque	any, any at all, some ... or other
altrui	another's, of other people

Note:

i) **ogni** is always used with singular nouns:

ogni giorno   **ogni madre**
every day   every mother

But: note the usage with numerals:

vado dal medico ogni sei mesi
I go to the doctor every six months

ii) **qualche** is always used with a singular noun and only with those nouns which could have a plural:

l'ho già incontrata qualche volta
I've already met her a few times

al largo si vedeva qualche barca a vela
offshore one could see a few sailing boats

For those nouns which do not have a plural, an expression such as **un po' di** must be used:

un po' di latte
some milk

iii) **qualsiasi** and **qualunque** are used with singular nouns and are interchangeable. When they follow the noun, they have the meaning of 'any at all', 'it doesn't matter which':

darei qualsiasi cosa per assistere alla partita
I would give anything to see the match

mi dia un giornale qualsiasi
give me any newspaper at all

è un uomo qualsiasi
he is just an ordinary man

pagherebbe qualunque prezzo per acquistare quel quadro
he/she'd pay any price to get that painting

qualunque cosa dicessi, non ti crederei
whatever you said, I wouldn't believe you

iv) **altrui** follows the noun:

non toccare la roba altrui
don't touch other people's things

3. Indefinite pronouns or adjectives

nessuno/a	no one, no
ciascuno/a	each one, everyone, each
alcuno/a/i/e	some
altro/a/i/e	another, other
troppo/a/i/e	too many, too much
molto/a/i/e	many, much
poco/poca/pochi/poche	few
tanto/a/i/e	so many, so much
quanto/a/i/e	as many, how many, how much
parecchio/a/i/e	several
tale/i	such
tutto/a/i/e	all, every
certo/a/i/e	certain

Note: the rules for the omission of the **o** in the indefinite adjectives **nessuno, ciascuno** and **alcuno** are the same as for **uno**, see p 20

quest'anno nessuno ha celebrato la festa
this year no one celebrated the festival

nessuna donna accetterebbe di essere trattata così
no woman would accept being treated like that

ho dato un regalo a ciascuno di loro
I gave them each a present

non fa altro che piangere
he/she does nothing but cry

si deve trovare un'altra soluzione
another solution must be found

a molti è parsa una decisione sbagliata
to many people it seemed like a wrong decision

molti spettatori sono stati feriti
many spectators were injured

pochi s'interessano a quell'argomento
few people are interested in that topic

siamo arrivati a casa poco tempo fa
we got home a little while ago

parecchi erano già andati via
several people had already left

mi sono rimaste parecchie cose da fare
I have several things left to do

c'è un tale che l'aspetta in ufficio
there's someone or other waiting for you in the office

una tale spiegazione non soddisferà mai il pubblico
such an explanation will never satisfy the public

a quell'incrocio succede un incidente tutte le settimane
every week there's an accident at those crossroads

non tutti possono permettersi il lusso di viaggiare
not everyone can afford to travel

Note:

i) **alcuno** can be used both in the singular and in the plural, but, if it occurs in an affirmative sentence, it must be in the plural:

ho letto alcuni libri di Calvino
I've read some books by Calvino

non ho alcun dubbio
I have no doubt(s)

alcuni piatti regionali sono facili da preparare
some regional dishes are easy to prepare

alcuni accettano la nuova tecnologia, altri no
some people accept new technology, others don't

ii) there are a number of idiomatic expressions involving **tutto**, one or two examples of which are given below:

Buon Natale a *tutti quanti*!
Happy Christmas to all of you!

sono contentissimi *tutti e due*
they are both very happy

iii) when the adjective **certo** precedes the noun it has the sense of 'some', 'some but not others', whereas after the noun it has the sense of 'sure' or 'indisputable':

certi voli sono stati rimandati a domani mattina
some flights have been postponed until tomorrow morning

certi si sono dichiarati contenti dei cambiamenti
certain people declared themselves happy with the changes

una certa signora Ferrari ha telefonato mezz'ora fa
a (certain) Signora Ferrari telephoned half an hour ago

è una cosa certa! vincerà la nostra squadra
it's a sure thing! our team will win

I. DEMONSTRATIVE PRONOUNS AND ADJECTIVES

1. *questo*

questo/a/i/e (this, these) functions either as a pronoun or as an adjective. Note that as an adjective, the final **-o** or **-a** can be dropped before a noun beginning with a vowel (especially if it is the same vowel):

di chi è questo?
whose is this?

questi sono i miei nipoti
these are my grandchildren

questi tulipani
these tulips

quest'aereo/questo aereo
this plane

questa ragazza
this girl

2. *quello*

quello/a/i/e (that, those) functions both as a pronoun and as an adjective but the forms are slightly different in each case:

a) The pronoun forms are **quello, quella, quelli** and **quelle**:

avevo dimenticato il mio ombrello, così ho preso quello di mio padre
I had forgotten my umbrella so I took my father's

preferiscono quelli bianchi
they prefer those white ones

b) The adjectival forms resemble those of the definite article:

quel libro that book	**quei libri** those books
quell'albergo that hotel	**quegli alberghi** those hotels
quello studente that student	**quegli studenti** those students

quella signora that lady | **quelle signore** those ladies
quell'agenzia that agency | **quelle agenzie** those agencies

3. *questo* and *quello*

a) Proximity and distance may be emphasized by the addition after the pronoun of the appropriate adverbs of place, **qui** and **qua** (here) or **lì** and **là** (there):

ti piace questo qui? - no, preferisco quello lì
do you like this one here? - no, I prefer that one there

questa qua mi sembra un po' amara
this one here seems to me to be slightly bitter

b) As pronouns, **questo** and **quello** may be employed in the construction, 'the former ... the latter' (note, however, that **questo** means 'the latter' and **quello** means 'the former'):

ho visto il cliente francese e quello giapponese: questo vuole venire senz'altro, ma quello non si è ancora deciso
I have seen the French and the Japanese customers: the latter definitely wants to come but the former hasn't decided yet

Note:

i) the latter (**questo/a/i/e**) is always mentioned first:

ii) one may use **il primo... il secondo** or **il primo... l'ultimo** instead of **questo... quello**:

Vialli e Lineker sono capicannonieri: il primo è italiano, il secondo inglese
Vialli and Lineker are leading goal scorers: the first is Italian and the second English

iii) there is also an older invariable form **questi... quegli** (the former ... the latter) which will be found in the literary language

4. *costui* and *colui*

Two other sets of demonstrative pronouns should be mentioned although their use is declining:

costui this man | **costei** this woman | **costoro** these people
colui that man | **colei** that woman | **coloro** those people

coloro che non vogliono entrare rimangano fuori
those who don't want to come in should stay outside

costui etc often have a derogatory meaning:

chi è costui?
who (on earth) is that fellow?

5. *ciò*

ciò (that) is an invariable neuter pronoun referring to objects or ideas mentioned previously:

ciò non è vero
that's not true

tutto ciò mi sorprende veramente
all that really surprises me

e con ciò?
so what?

6. *stesso* and *medesimo*

stesso and **medesimo** mean 'same' and agree with their subject (the former is more common in the spoken language):

frequentiamo lo stesso circolo sportivo
we go to the same sports club

stesso, however, can also be used as a reinforcing word, in which case it always follows the noun or pronoun:

il direttore stesso non sa che fare
the director himself doesn't know what to do

l'ho vista io stesso
I saw her myself

è partita la sera stessa
she left that very evening

ama solo se stesso
he loves only himself

J. RELATIVE PRONOUNS

1. *che*

a) **che** means 'who', 'whom', 'which' and 'that' and is invariable. It refers to both people and things. It may be used only with the function of a subject or of a direct object pronoun:

il ragazzo che ha gridato
the boy who shouted

sono persone che conosco da parecchi anni
they are people whom I've known for several years

questo è il romanzo che ha vinto il premio Strega
this is the novel that (which) won the Strega prize

Note: the relative pronoun may *not* be omitted in Italian as it quite
often is in English:

la lavastoviglie che ho comprato l'anno scorso
the dishwasher I bought last year

la ragazza che ho visto
the girl I saw

For the agreement of the past participle after a relative pronoun see
p 158.

b) *il che*

che is occasionally preceded by the article -**il** - thus acquiring the
sense 'something which', 'this':

è stata molto ammalata, il che mi ha fatto pena
she was very ill, which upset me

Note: **ha chiesto di mia madre, del che ero molto grato**
he/she asked after my mother, for which I was very grateful

c) *quel che, quello che and ciò che*

quel che, quello che and **ciò che** are all relative pronouns meaning
'what'. They refer to things, not persons, and are interchangeable:

raccontami quel che (ciò che) hai fatto
tell me what you've been doing

mangio ciò che voglio
I eat what I like

non riusciamo a sentire quello che dici
we can't hear what you're saying

Note: 'all that' is translated by **tutto quel (quello, ciò) che**. English is
very apt to miss out the relative pronoun in a way that is
impossible in Italian:

ecco tutto quel che posso dirle
that's all I can tell you/her

2. *cui* **as a pronoun**

a) Since the relative pronoun **che** may be used only as a subject or a direct object pronoun, with a preposition it is necessary to substitute the invariable pronoun **cui**:

> **il pianista di cui ti ho parlato tanto**
> the pianist I have so often told you about

> **la signora con cui sono andato al concerto**
> the lady with whom I went to the concert

> **la ragione per cui ho rifiutato è questa**
> this is the reason I refused

b) the preposition **a** before **cui** meaning 'to which', 'to whom' can be omitted:

> **questo è il progetto (a) cui ho preso parte**
> this is the project I took part in

3. *cui* **as a possessive**

cui meaning 'whose', 'of whom' or 'of which' is invariable. It is positioned between the definite article and the noun:

> **questa è la signora il cui figlio è gravemente malato**
> this is the lady whose son is seriously ill

> **è un paese i cui costumi mi sono totalmente sconosciuti**
> it is a country whose customs (the customs of which) are totally unknown to me

> **qui ci sono ville i cui proprietari abitano all'estero**
> here there are villas whose owners live abroad

4. *il quale*

The pronouns **cui** and **che** may be substituted by **il quale** (**la quale/i quali/le quali**). These pronouns refer both to people and things and agree in number and gender with the subject.

a) As a substitute for **che**, **il quale** is usually employed only in order to avoid ambiguity:

> **la moglie del signor Galli, la quale ha organizzato quella gita a San Gimignano**
> Signor Galli's wife who organized that trip to San Gimignano

b) When substituted for **cui** preceded by a preposition, the examples given in section 2 above would become:

> **il pianista del quale ti ho parlato tanto**
> the pianist I have so often told you about

> **la signora con la quale sono andato al concerto**
> the lady with whom I went to the concert

> **la ragione per la quale ho rifiutato è questa**
> this is the reason I refused

c) When substituted for **cui** in its possessive function, the examples given in section 3 above would become:

> **questa è la signora il figlio della quale è gravemente malato**
> this is the lady whose son is seriously ill

> **è un paese i costumi del quale mi sono totalmente sconosciuti**
> it is a country whose customs are totally unknown to me

> **qui ci sono ville i proprietari delle quali abitano all'estero**
> here there are villas whose owners live abroad

5. *chi*

chi is an invariable pronoun which has two meanings: 'the one/ones who' and 'anyone who'. It refers only to people and must be followed by a singular verb. It is commonly used in proverbs:

> **chi vuole andare al mare con questo freddo è pazzo**
> anyone who wants to go to the seaside in this cold is mad

> **non riesco a trovare chi mi accompagnerà dal dentista**
> I can't find anyone who will go with me to the dentist's

> **non sappiamo a chi rivolgerci per avere le chiavi**
> we don't know who to go to to get the keys

> **chi vivrà, vedrà**
> only time will tell

> **ride bene chi ride ultimo**
> he who laughs last laughs longest

K. INTERROGATIVE AND EXCLAMATORY PRONOUNS AND ADJECTIVES

Interrogative pronouns and adjectives are used in direct and indirect questions. Some words can function both as pronouns and as adjectives:

1. Interrogative pronouns

a) **chi** 'who', is an invariable interrogative pronoun which refers only to people:

> **chi ve l'ha detto?**
> who told you?
>
> **con chi hai cenato?**
> who did you have dinner with?
>
> **di chi è questa bici?**
> whose bike is this?
>
> **dimmi chi sei**
> tell me who you are

b) **che, che cosa, cosa** 'what' are invariable interrogative pronouns which refer only to things:

> **che hai detto?**
> what did you say?
>
> **che cosa c'è da vedere?**
> what is there to see?
>
> **cosa stai facendo?**
> what are you doing?
>
> **ditemi che cosa avete visto**
> tell me what you saw

Note: the use of **cosa** without **che** would be less appropriate in a more formal context

c) **quale/i** 'which (one/ones)' is an interrogative pronoun which refers both to people and to things:

> **quale preferisce, signora?**
> which one do you prefer, Madam?
>
> **quali vuoi buttar via?**
> which ones do you want to throw out?
>
> **qual è il vostro cantante preferito?**
> who is your favourite singer?
>
> **qual è la tua camera?**
> which is your bedroom?
>
> **mi ha chiesto qual era il significato di questo**
> he asked me what the meaning of this was

d) **quanto/a/i/e** 'how much', 'how many':

> **quanto hai pagato quelle scarpe?**
> how much did you pay for those shoes?

> **mi dica quanto le devo, signore**
> tell me how much I owe you, sir

> **quante ne hai incontrato/e?**
> how many of them did you meet?

2. Interrogative adjectives

a) **che** 'what' is invariable:

> **che tipo di vacanze ti piace di più?**
> what sort of holiday do you like best?

> **che programma vuoi guardare?**
> what programme do you want to watch?

b) **quale/i** 'what', 'which (one/ones)':

> **per quale motivo hai convocato questa riunione?**
> for what reason did you call this meeting?

> **quale camicetta ti metti stamattina?**
> which blouse are you putting on this morning?

> **quali alberghi ci sono nei dintorni?**
> what hotels are there round here?

c) **quanto/a/i/e** 'how much', 'how many':

> **quante università ci sono adesso in Italia?**
> how many universities are there now in Italy?

> **quanta disoccupazione c'è attualmente in Gran Bretagna?**
> how much unemployment is there at present in Great Britain?

3. Exclamatory uses of *che, come* and *quanto*

che brutta giornata!	what a horrible day!
che bello!	how lovely!
che puzza!	what a stink!
che fame!	I'm so hungry!
che noia!	how boring!
come sei gentile!	how nice of you!
come sei seccante!	how annoying you are!
quanta gente!	what a crowd!
quante storie!	what a lot of nonsense!

7. VERBS

A. REGULAR CONJUGATIONS

1. Conjugations

There are three conjugations in Italian, which are determined by the infinitive endings. The first conjugation verbs, the largest category, end in **-are** (eg **parlare**) and will be referred to as **-are** verbs; the second conjugation verbs end in **-ere** (eg **credere**) and will be referred to as **-ere** verbs; the third conjugation verbs, the smallest category, end in **-ire** (eg **sentire**) and will be referred to as **-ire** verbs.

2. Simple tenses

The simple tenses in Italian are:

a) present
b) imperfect
c) future
d) conditional
e) past historic
f) present subjunctive
g) imperfect subjunctive

For the uses of the different tenses, see pp 123-30.

3. Formation of tenses

The tenses are formed by adding the following endings to the stem of the infinitive as set out in the following section:

a) *PRESENT*: stem of the infinitive + the following endings:

-are VERBS	**-ere** VERBS
-o, -i, -a,	-o, -i, -e
-iamo, -ate, -ano	-iamo, -ete, -ono
PARL*ARE*	**CRED*ERE***
parlo	credo
parli	credi

parla	crede
parliamo	crediamo
parlate	credete
parlano	credono

Note: verbs in **-ere** can have a stressed ending (eg **vedere**) or unstressed (eg **credere**). Their conjugation remains the same.

-ire VERBS

-o, -i, -e,	-isco, -isci, -isce
-iamo, -ite, -ono	-iamo, -ite, -iscono

SENTIRE	**CAPIRE**
sento	capisco
senti	capisci
sente	capisce
sentiamo	capiamo
sentite	capite
sentono	capiscono

Note:
1) as seen above, many verbs of the third conjugation insert **-isc-** between the stem and the ending in the singular and in the third person plural of the present indicative and subjunctive. The most common ones are: **capire** (to understand), **costruire** (to build), **finire** (to finish), **preferire** (to prefer), **pulire** (to clean).

ii) the stress of the third person plural of the three conjugations always falls on the root of the verb and *never* on the ending, for example:

capiscono

b) *IMPERFECT*: stem of the infinitive + the following endings:

-are VERBS	-ere VERBS	-ire VERBS
-avo, -avi, -ava,	-evo, -evi, -eva,	- ivo, -ivi, -iva
-avamo, -avate,	-evamo, -evate,	-ivamo, -ivate, -ivano
-avano	-evano	
parlavo	credevo	sentivo
parlavi	credevi	sentivi
parlava	credeva	sentiva
parlavamo	credevamo	sentivamo
parlavate	credevate	sentivate
parlavano	credevano	sentivano

c) *FUTURE*: infinitive removing the final **-e** + the following endings:

   -ò, -ai, -à, -emo, -ete, -anno

Note: regular verbs in **-are** change the characteristic vowel **a** into **e**:

parlerò	crederò	sentirò
parlerai	crederai	sentirai
parlerà	crederà	sentirà
parleremo	crederemo	sentiremo
parlerete	crederete	sentirete
parleranno	crederanno	sentiranno

d) *CONDITIONAL*: stem of the future + the following endings:

   -ei, -esti, -ebbe, -emmo, -este, -ebbero

parlerei	crederei	sentirei
parleresti	crederesti	sentiresti
parlerebbe	crederebbe	sentirebbe
parleremmo	crederemmo	sentiremmo
parlereste	credereste	sentireste
parlerebbero	crederebbero	sentirebbero

e) *PAST HISTORIC*: stem of the infinitive + the following endings:

-are VERBS	**-ere** VERBS	**-ire** VERBS
-ai, -asti, -ò	**-ei, -esti, -è**	**-ii, -isti, -ì**
-ammo, -aste,	**-emmo, -este,**	**-immo, -iste, -irono**
-arono	**-erono**	
parlai	credei	sentii
parlasti	credesti	sentisti
parlò	credè	sentì
parlammo	credemmo	sentimmo
parlaste	credeste	sentiste
parlarono	crederono	sentirono

Note: for most verbs in **-ere** (but not those whose root ends in **t**, like **potere**) there are alternative forms for the first person singular and the third person singular and plural: **-etti, -ette, -ettero** (eg **credetti, credette, credettero**). These forms are used just as frequently.

f) *PRESENT SUBJUNCTIVE*: stem of the infinitive + the following endings:

-are VERBS	-ere VERBS	-ire VERBS
-i, -i, -i,	-a, -a, -a,	-a, -a, -a,
-iamo, -iate, -ino	-iamo, -iate, -ano	- iamo, -iate, -ano
parli	creda	senta
parli	creda	senta
parli	creda	senta
parliamo	crediamo	sentiamo
parliate	crediate	sentiate
parlino	credano	sentano

g) *IMPERFECT SUBJUNCTIVE*: stem of the infinitive + the following endings:

-are VERBS	-ere VERBS	-ire VERBS
-assi, -assi, -asse,	-essi, -essi, -esse,	-issi, -issi, -isse,
-assimo, -aste,	-essimo, -este,	-issimo, -iste,
-assero	-essero	-issero
amassi	credessi	sentissi
amassi	credessi	sentissi
amasse	credesse	sentisse
amassimo	credessimo	sentissimo
amaste	credeste	sentiste
amassero	credessero	sentissero

For the conjugation of the auxiliary verbs **essere** (to be) and **avere** (to have) and of the main irregular verbs, see pp 169-88.

B. STANDARD SPELLING IRREGULARITIES

In some first conjugation verbs, spelling changes occur to ensure that the pronunciation remains the same throughout the conjugation:

1. First conjugation verbs in *-care* and *-gare*

Verbs in **-care** and **-gare** retain the same sound which the **c** and **g** have in the infinitive by inserting an **h** before **i** and **e**:

cerco	cercherò	pago	pagherò
cerchi	cercherai	paghi	pagherai
cerca	cercherà	paga	pagherà
cerchiamo	cercheremo	paghiamo	pagheremo
cercate	cercherete	pagate	pagherete
cercano	cercheranno	pagano	pagheranno

2. Verbs in *-ciare*, *-giare* and *-sciare*

Verbs in **-ciare**, **-giare** and **-sciare** drop the **i** of the stem whenever it precedes **i** and **e**:

comincio	comincerò	mangio	mangerò
cominci	comincerai	mangi	mangerai
comincia	comincerà	mangia	mangerà
cominciamo	cominceremo	mangiamo	mangeremo
cominciate	comincerete	mangiate	mangerete
cominciano	cominceranno	mangiano	mangeranno

lascio	lascerò
lasci	lascerai
lascia	lascerà
lasciamo	lasceremo
lasciate	lascerete
lasciano	lasceranno

3. Verbs in *-gnare*

Verbs in **-gnare** keep the **i** when it is part of the ending, ie in the first person plural of the present indicative and in the first and second persons plural of the present subjunctive:

bagniamo, bagnate (*pres ind*)
bagniamo, bagniate (*pres subj*)

4. **Verbs in** *-gliare*

Verbs in **-gliare** keep the **i** before **o**, **a** and **e** but drop it before another **i**:

> **sbadiglio**
> **sbadiglia**
> **sbadiglierei** (*cond*)
> **sbadigli** (*pres subj*)

5. **Verbs in** *-iare*

Verbs in **-iare** retain the **i** of the stem if this **i** is stressed, but they lose it otherwise:

scio (stressed)	**cambio** (unstressed)
scii	**cambi**
scia	**cambia**
sciamo	**cambiamo**
sciate	**cambiate**
sciano	**cambiano**

6. **Second conjugation verbs in** *-cere, -gere, -scere*

Verbs in **-cere**, **-gere** and **-scere** change the pronunciation of the last consonant of the stem according to the first vowel of the ending:

vinco	**leggo**	**conosco**
vinci	**leggi**	**conosci**
vince	**legge**	**conosce**
vinciamo	**leggiamo**	**conosciamo**
vincete	**leggete**	**conoscete**
vincono	**leggono**	**conoscono**

Note:

i) **fuggire** (third conjugation) (to escape) also behaves in the same way: **fuggo, fuggi, fugge, fuggiamo, fuggite, fuggono**

ii) *exceptions*: **cuocere** (to cook) and **cucire** (third conjugation) (to sew) retain the 'soft' sound of the infinitive throughout:

cuocio	**cucio**
cuoci	**cuci**
cuoce	**cuce**

cuociamo
cuocete
cuociono

cuciamo
cucite
cuciono

C. AUXILIARIES AND THE FORMATION OF COMPOUND TENSES

1. Formation

a) The two auxiliary verbs **avere** and **essere** are used with the past participle of a verb to form compound tenses.

b) *The past participle*

The regular past participle is formed by taking the stem of the infinitive and adding the following endings:

-are VERBS	-ere VERBS	-ire VERBS
parl(are) + ato	cred(ere) + uto	sent(ire) + ito
parlato	creduto	sentito

For the agreement of past participles see pp 158-9.

c) *Compound tenses*

In Italian there are seven compound tenses: perfect, pluperfect, future perfect, past conditional (perfect conditional), past anterior, perfect subjunctive and pluperfect subjunctive.

2. Verbs conjugated with *AVERE*

a) *PERFECT*	b) *PLUPERFECT*
present of **avere** + past participle	imperfect of **avere** + past participle
ho parlato	avevo parlato
hai parlato	avevi parlato
ha parlato	aveva parlato
abbiamo parlato	avevamo parlato
avete parlato	avevate parlato
hanno parlato	avevano parlato

c) *FUTURE PERFECT*

future of **avere** +
past participle

avrò parlato
avrai parlato
avrà parlato
avremo parlato
avrete parlato
avranno parlato

d) *PAST CONDITIONAL*

conditional of **avere** +
past participle

avrei parlato
avresti parlato
avrebbe parlato
avremmo parlato
avreste parlato
avrebbero parlato

e) *PAST ANTERIOR*

past historic of **avere** +
past participle

ebbi parlato
avesti parlato
ebbe parlato
avemmo parlato
aveste parlato
ebbero parlato

f) *PERFECT SUBJUNCTIVE*

present subjunctive of
avere + past participle

abbia parlato
abbia parlato
abbia parlato
abbiamo parlato
abbiate parlato
abbiano parlato

g) *PLUPERFECT SUBJUNCTIVE*

imperfect subjunctive of
avere + past participle

avessi parlato
avessi parlato
avesse parlato
avessimo parlato
aveste parlato
avessero parlato

3. Verbs conjugated with *ESSERE*

a) *PERFECT*

present of **essere** +
past participle

sono arrivato/a
sei arrivato/a
è arrivato/a
siamo arrivati/e
siete arrivati/e
sono arrivati/e

b) *PLUPERFECT*

imperfect of **essere** +
past participle

ero arrivato/a
eri arrivato/a
era arrivato/a
eravamo arrivati/e
eravate arrivati/c
erano arrivati/e

c) *FUTURE PERFECT*

future of **essere** +
past participle

sarò arrivato/a
sarai arrivato/a
sarà arrivato/a
saremo arrivati/e
sarete arrivati/e
saranno arrivati/e

d) *PAST CONDITIONAL*

conditional of **essere** +
past participle

sarei arrivato/a
saresti arrivato/a
sarebbe arrivato/a
saremmo arrivati/e
sareste arrivati/e
sarebbero arrivati/e

e) *PAST ANTERIOR*

past historic of **essere** +
past participle

fui arrivato/a
fosti arrivato/a
fu arrivato/a
fummo arrivati/e
foste arrivati/e
furono arrivati/e

f) *PERFECT SUBJUNCTIVE*

present subjunctive of
essere + past participle

sia arrivato/a
sia arrivato/a
sia arrivato/a
siamo arrivati/e
siate arrivati/e
siano arrivati/e

g) *PLUPERFECT SUBJUNCTIVE*

imperfect subjunctive of
essere + past participle

fossi arrivato/a
fossi arrivato/a
fosse arrivato/a
fossimo arrivati/e
foste arrivati/e
fossero arrivati/e

4. *AVERE* or *ESSERE*?

a) *Verbs conjugated with avere*

The compound tenses of most verbs (and all transitive verbs) are formed with **avere**:

ho parlato italiano tutto il giorno
I spoke Italian all day

Pietro ha fumato per dieci anni e poi ha smesso
Pietro smoked for ten years and then he stopped

b) *Verbs conjugated with essere*

i) all reflexive verbs (see p 116):

mi sono divertito molto
I enjoyed myself very much

ii) some verbs that indicate movement or staying:

andare	to go
arrivare	to arrive
cadere	to fall
emigrare	to emigrate
entrare	to enter
fuggire	to escape
partire	to leave
passare	to go through, to drop in
restare	to stay
rimanere	to remain
sorgere	to rise
tornare	to return
uscire	to go out
venire	to come

era emigrato negli anni sessanta ma ora è tornato
he emigrated in the sixties but now he is back

non è ancora passato a salutarci
he has not yet dropped in to say hello

è rimasta solo dieci minuti e poi è uscita
she stayed only ten minutes and then she went out

iii) verbs which indicate changes or psychological or physical processes linked with the subject:

apparire/comparire	to appear
arrossire	to blush

dimagrire	to lose weight
divenire/diventare	to become
essere	to be
impallidire	to turn pale
impazzire	to go mad
ingrassare	to put on weight
marcire	to rot
morire	to die
nascere	to be born
parere/sembrare	to seem
scomparire	to disappear
scoppiare	to blow up

è ingrassato molto da quando è andato in pensione
he has put on a lot of weight since he retired

non mi è sembrato giusto dirglielo
it did not seem right to tell him about it

Note: notice the difference between English and Italian in the use of tenses with **nascere**:

sono nato nel 1970
I was born in 1970

iv) the verb **piacere** and the following verbs, which are similar to **piacere** in their construction:

bastare	to be sufficient
dispiacere	to be sorry
importare	to matter
mancare	to lack, to miss
occorrere/servire	to be necessary

Note: the construction of these verbs in Italian is different from English: they take an indirect object followed by the verb and by the subject:

non mi è mai piaciuto il suo atteggiamento
I never liked his/her/your attitude

le è bastato uno sguardo
one look was enough for her

non gli è mai mancato il coraggio
he never lacked courage

v) impersonal verbs:

accadere
capitare   to happen
succedere

mi è capitato spesso di incontrarlo ai giardini
I often happened to come across him in the park

Note: impersonal verbs referring to the weather can take either auxiliary: **è/ha piovuto** (it has rained), **era/aveva nevicato** (it had snowed), etc.

vi) other verbs:

costare	to cost
dipendere	to depend
esistere	to exist
intervenire	to intervene
prevalere	to prevail
ricorrere	to turn to
risultare	to result
riuscire	to succeed
valere	to be worth
volerci	to take, to require

il suo nuovo impianto stereo gli è costato un occhio della testa
his new hi-fi cost him a bomb

non erano affatto intervenuti nella faccenda
they had not intervened at all in the matter

sono ricorso al loro aiuto più volte
I have turned to them many times for help

ci è voluta tutta la mia pazienza per convincerla
it took a lot of patience to convince her

c) *Verbs which can take either **essere** or **avere***

Some verbs take **avere** when they have an object, **essere** when they do not. Here are some of the most common ones:

aumentare	to increase
cessare/smettere	to stop
cominciare	to start
continuare	to continue
diminuire	to diminish
finire	to finish
guarire	to cure, to recover

migliorare	to improve
salire	to go up
scendere	to go down
seguire	to follow
servire	to serve, to be necessary
vivere	to live

il pilota ha aumentato la velocità
the pilot increased speed

recentemente i prezzi sono aumentati
recently prices have gone up

ho cambiato la macchina l'anno scorso
I changed my car last year

tutti i numeri telefonici di Londra sono cambiati
all London telephone numbers have changed

hanno migliorato la qualità dei videoregistratori
they have improved the quality of videos

la mia salute è migliorata con la ginnastica
my health has improved with exercise

Note: some of these verbs can take a preposition + infinitive; in this
case their auxiliary is always **avere**:

ho cominciato a studiare due ore fa
I started studying two hours ago

hanno finito di riparare la lavatrice?
have they finished repairing the washing-machine?

d) *Verbs which have a different meaning, according to the auxiliary*

convenire	to agree/to gather
correre	to run/to run somewhere
mancare	to lack, to neglect/to be lacking, to be missing

i sindacati hanno convenuto che lo sciopero era necessario
the trade unions have agreed that the strike was necessary

i partecipanti erano convenuti da ogni parte d'Italia
the participants had gathered from every part of Italy

in quell'occasione hai mancato di tatto
on that occasion you lacked tact

sei mancato agli appuntamenti troppe volte
you have missed your appointments too often

Note:
  i)   **correre, saltare** and **volare** usually take **avere**, but they take **essere** when they are followed by a specification of place:

      ha corso finché non gli è mancato il fiato
      he ran until he was out of breath

      è corso alla stazione ma non è arrivato in tempo
      he ran to the station but he did not make it in time

  ii)   **volare** also takes **essere** when its subject indicates a length of time:

      le ferie quest'anno sono volate!
      the holidays really flew by this year!

      il tempo era proprio volato
      time had really flown

e)   *Verbs which can take either auxiliary, with no change in meaning*

      | | |
      appartenere   to belong
      giovare   to be useful, to be good
      vivere   to live

      ha/è appartenuto a quell'associazione per anni
      he belonged to that society for years

      le ha giovato/le è giovata molto l'aria di mare
      the sea air was very good for her

      hai/sei vissuto in questa casa per troppo tempo
      you have lived in this house too long

Note: modal verbs (ie **dovere, potere** and **volere**) accompanying an infinitive requiring **essere** normally take **essere** too, but the form with **avere** is also used:

      non è potuta (ha potuto) andare alla riunione
      she could not go to the meeting

      non sono potuto (ho potuto) rimanere perché non avevo più una lira
      I could not stay because I had no money left

D. REFLEXIVE VERBS

1. Definition

Reflexive verbs are so called because they 'reflect' the action back onto the subject. Reflexive verbs are always accompanied by a reflexive pronoun, for example in the sentence 'I washed myself with soap', 'myself' is a reflexive pronoun.

non-reflexive	*reflexive*
lavo la macchina ogni settimana	**mi lavo**
I wash the car every week	I wash myself

2. Reflexive pronouns

They are:

PERSON	SINGULAR	PLURAL
1st	**mi** myself	**ci** ourselves
2nd	**ti** yourself	**vi** yourselves
3rd	**si** himself, herself, itself, oneself, yourself (*polite*)	**si** themselves, yourselves (*polite*)

Note:

i) Italian reflexive pronouns are often not translated in English:

mi chiedo se...	**si prendono gioco di me**
I wonder if ...	they 're making fun of me

ii) in a dictionary you will find reflexive verbs in the infinitive with the reflexive pronoun **si** replacing the final **e**:

lavar-e	to wash
lavar-si	to wash oneself
difender-e	to defend
difender-si	to defend oneself

3. Conjugation of reflexive verbs

a) *Simple tenses*

These are formed in the same way as for non-reflexive verbs, except that a reflexive pronoun is also present.

b) *Compound tenses*

These are formed with the auxiliary **essere** followed by the past participle of the verb.

A full conjugation table is given on p 180. For agreement of reflexive verbs see p 159.

4.   Position of reflexive pronouns

The position of reflexive pronouns is the same as for all other unstressed personal pronouns: they always precede the verb except in the second persons of the imperative and in the non-finite forms of the verb (eg infinitive, gerund and participle). In the negative form of the second person singular and plural of the imperative the pronoun can either precede or follow the verb:

la sposa si è vestita da sola
the bride got dressed without help

vestiti!
get dressed!

voleva vestirsi da sola
she wanted to get dressed on her own

vestendosi si guardava allo specchio
while getting dressed he/she looked at himself/herself in the mirror

vestitasi, partì per la chiesa
having got dressed, she left for church

non vestirti!/non ti vestire!
don't get dressed!

5.   Types of reflexive verbs

a) Verbs in which the action reflects back onto the subject, equivalent to English reflexive constructions with '-self':

ti lavi	**si è ucciso**	**vi servite**
you wash yourself	he killed himself	you help yourselves

b) Verbs which are followed by a direct object; in this case the reflexive pronoun has the function of an indirect object (eg it means 'to/for me, to/for you', etc):

mi sono comprata un videoregistratore
I bought myself a video

ci siamo preparate la cena in mezz'ora
we prepared the dinner (for ourselves) in half an hour

c) Many transitive verbs can be used reflexively to indicate a reciprocal action, usually translated in English with 'each other' or 'one another':

amarsi	to love	
baciarsi	to kiss	
conoscersi	to know	each other/one another
odiarsi	to hate	
scriversi	to write to	

si conoscono da quando erano bambini
they have known each other since they were children

si scrivono regolarmente
they write to each other regularly

d) Verbs which indicate movement of the body. In English they would be translated with intransitive verbs followed by an adverb (eg 'to lean over', 'to climb up', etc):

alzarsi	to get up
affacciarsi	to lean out
arrampicarsi	to climb up
chinarsi	to lean down
coricarsi	to lie down
muoversi	to move
sedersi	to sit down
spostarsi	to move

Note: some of these verbs can also have the normal transitive function:

ho alzato il vaso per vedere cosa c'era sotto
I lifted the vase to see what was underneath

ho mosso la pedina troppo presto
I moved my pawn too soon

e) Verbs which denote physiological or psychological processes, often translated in English with 'to get' or 'to become' followed by an adjective:

addormentarsi	to fall asleep
affezionarsi a	to become fond of
ammalarsi	to become ill
annoiarsi	to get bored

arrabbiarsi	to get angry
confondersi	to get mixed up
divertirsi	to enjoy oneself
offendersi	to get offended
pentirsi	to regret/to repent
svegliarsi	to wake up
vergognarsi	to be ashamed

si affezionò molto a quel cane
he/she became very fond of that dog

mi sono annoiata mortalmente a quella festa
I got terribly bored at that party

non ti vergogni di quello che hai fatto?
are you not ashamed of what you have done?

Note: some of these verbs can have a normal transitive function:

ho addormentato mio figlio con una ninna-nanna
I sang my son to sleep with a lullaby

ha confuso la madre con la figlia
he/she mistook the mother for the daughter

But: notice the alternative transitive and reflexive forms of the verbs
dimenticare and **ricordare**:

ricordo molto bene quella ragazza
I remember that girl very well

mi ricordo molto bene di quella ragazza
I remember that girl very well

dimentico sempre quello che devo comprare
I always forget what I have to buy

mi dimentico sempre di quello che devo comprare
I always forget what I have to buy

f)   Verbs which are used in the reflexive form as an alternative to their
     normal transitive form, normally in colloquial Italian, without any
     substantial difference in their meaning:

ci siamo mangiati un bel piatto di pastasciutta
we ate a good dish of pasta

non me lo sogno nemmeno!
I wouldn't dream of it!

appena alzata mi bevo una tazza di caffè
as soon as I get up I drink a cup of coffee

E. IMPERSONAL VERBS

Impersonal verbs in English are always in the third person singular and take 'it' for their subject. In Italian they are more complicated than in English and can be grouped in the following way:

1. Verbs and phrases describing the weather:

a) **fare** + adjective:

fa bello/caldo it's fine/warm	**fa fresco/freddo** it's cool/cold
domani farà bello the weather will be good tomorrow	**fa molto freddo** it's very cold

b) **fare** + noun:

fa bel tempo the weather is nice	**fa brutto tempo** the weather is bad

Note:

i)

fa giorno it's daylight	**fa notte** it's dark

ii) instead of the impersonal expressions **fa bel/brutto tempo**, one can also use **il tempo è bello/brutto**.

c) Other impersonal verbs and verbs used impersonally to describe the weather:

gela	**(gelare)**	it's freezing
grandina	**(grandinare)**	it's hailing
nevica	**(nevicare)**	it's snowing
piove	**(piovere)**	it's raining
tuona	**(tuonare)**	it's thundering
tira vento	**(tirare vento)**	it's windy

Note: some of these can be used personally:

    sto gelando   I am freezing

2. Impersonal expressions formed with **essere** followed by an adjective:

è difficile	it's difficult
è facile	it's easy
è necessario	it's necessary

è inutile	it's useless
è possibile	it's possible
è sufficiente	it's sufficient

è difficile parlarne
it's difficult to talk about it

è necessario che tu sia presente
it is necessary for you to be present

For the use of the subjunctive see p 133.

3. Verbs expressing pleasure/displeasure, need/lack etc are followed by a dependent clause whose verb can be a subjunctive or an infinitive, depending on whether the subject of the second verb is mentioned (see rules of the subjunctive pp 132-3):

a) *piacere (to like)*, *dispiacere/rincrescere (to regret, to be sorry)*

non mi piace che frequenti quel ragazzo
I don't like you going out with that young man

mi è rincresciuto molto dover rinunciare alla festa
I was very sorry to have to miss the party

Note: these verbs can have a personal construction when accompanied by a noun which is their subject:

vi piacciono le macchine sportive?
do you like sports cars?

l'ultimo modello della FIAT non mi dispiace affatto
I don't dislike the latest FIAT model at all

tu piaci molto al professore
the teacher likes you a lot

b) *accadere, avvenire, succedere (to happen)*

accadeva spesso che la incontrasse in centro
it often happened that he/she met her in town

succede ogni tanto che la mia stampante si fermi
it sometimes happens that my printer stops

Note: personal construction:

è accaduta una disgrazia
there has been an accident

che è successo?
what happened?

c) ***bastare*** *(to be enough)*, ***restare*** *(to be left, to remain)*, ***mancare*** *(to be missing/lacking)*, ***servire/occorrere*** *(to be necessary)*

> **basta seguire le istruzioni**
> it is sufficient to follow the instructions

> **non mi resta che piangere**
> all I can do now is cry

> **manca solo che ti dimentichi di venire!**
> all we need now is for you to forget to come!

> **occorre sbrinare il frigo ogni tanto**
> it's necessary to defrost the fridge every now and then

Note: personal construction:

> **queste sedie non basteranno per tutti**
> these chairs won't be enough for everybody

> **che cosa manca per la cena di domani?**
> what is missing for tomorrow's dinner?

d) ***parere/sembrare*** *(to seem)*

> **pare che vada a trovare i figli ogni week-end**
> it seems that he/she goes to see his/her children every weekend

> **mi sembrava strano che non avesse capito**
> I thought it was curious that he/she hadn't understood

Note: personal construction:

> **dopo l'incidente pare/sembra invecchiato di dieci anni**
> after his accident he looks ten years older

4. Other common impersonal verbs:

a) ***trattarsi di*** *(to be a matter of)*

This may be followed by a noun, a pronoun or an infinitive:

> **si tratta del tuo avvenire**
> it's about your future

> **di che cosa si tratta?**
> what is it about?

> **si tratta di scoprire chi l'ha fatto**
> we must find who did it

b) *bisognare* *(to be necessary)*

> **bisogna che tu parta immediatamente**
> you must leave immediately

> **non bisogna perdere la calma**
> one must keep calm

Note: the verb **bisognare** is only used in the third person singular; for other persons use **avere bisogno di**:

> **ho bisogno di un nuovo nastro per la stampante**
> I need a new ribbon for my printer

> **non ha mai bisogno di aiuto**
> he/she never needs help

c) *volerci* *(to be necessary)* must be used in the third person plural when it refers to a plural

> **ci vuole molta pazienza per sopportarti!**
> it takes a lot of patience to put up with you!

> **per andare da Genova a Milano ci vogliono due ore di macchina**
> from Genoa to Milan it takes two hours by car

F. USE OF TENSES

For the formation of the various tenses see pp 100-3 and 107-14.

1. Present

The present is used to describe what someone does/something that happens regularly, or what someone is doing/something that is happening at the time of speaking.

a) *Present states*

> **sto bene**
> I'm well

b) *Regular actions*

> **lavora in fabbrica**
> he/she works in a factory
>
> **vado raramente al cinema**
> I seldom go to the cinema

c) *Actions which take place at the time of speaking*

> **dove vai? - vado di sopra**
> where are you going? - I'm going upstairs
>
> **che cosa fai? - controllo il motore**
> what are you doing? - I'm checking the engine

Note: notice the following two constructions with the verb **stare**:

i) **stare** + *gerund* corresponds to the English present progressive 'to be ... -ing':

> **sto leggendo l'ultimo libro di Moravia**
> I'm reading Moravia's latest book

ii) **stare** + **per** + *infinitive* corresponds to the English 'to be about to ...':

> **l'aereo sta per atterrare**
> the plane is about to land

d) *General truths and proverbs*

> **l'oro è un metallo prezioso**
> gold is a precious metal

non è tutto oro quel che luccica
all that glistens is not gold

e)   *Imminent or programmed future actions*

fra un anno mi sposo
I'm getting married in a year

domani c'è un programma interessante alla TV
there's an interesting programme on TV tomorrow

esco fra un'ora
I'm going out in an hour

torno subito
I'll be right back

f)   The present tense can be used in written Italian as an alternative to
the past historic to indicate past actions referring to historical or
literary events, giving them a more immediate and lively tone:

il 25 aprile 1945 gli Alleati liberano Milano e Genova
on April 25th 1945 the Allies liberated Milan and Genoa

la scoperta dell'America segna l'inizio dell'età moderna
the discovery of America marks the beginning of the modern age

g)   The present tense is used to render the English present perfect when
an action which started in the past is still continuing (see also
pp 126-7):

studio l'inglese da due anni
I have been studying English for two years

non fuma da più di un mese
he/she hasn't smoked for more than a month

2.   Imperfect

The imperfect is a past tense used to express what someone was
doing or what someone used to do or to describe something in the
past. The imperfect refers particularly to something that *continued*
over a period of time, as opposed to something that happened at a
specific point in time.

a)   *Continuous actions*

The imperfect describes an action that was happening when
something else took place (imperfect means unfinished):

leggeva un giornale quando è suonato il campanello
he/she was reading a newspaper when the bell rang

b) *Repeated or regular actions in the past*

> **la incontravo spesso in Via Roma**
> I often met her in Via Roma

> **quando lavoravo in quella ditta mi stancavo molto**
> I used to get very tired when I worked for that firm

c) *Descriptions in the past*

> **c'era una bella vista sul mare**
> there was a beautiful view of the sea

> **l'acqua di quel lago era sempre limpida**
> the water in the lake was always clear

> **il tempo era brutto quel giorno**
> the weather was bad that day

> **aveva i capelli biondi e gli occhi azzurri**
> he/she had fair hair and blue eyes

Note: the following two constructions with the verb **stare**:

i)   **stare** + *gerund* corresponds to the English past progressive 'to be ... -ing':

> **stava guardando il suo programma preferito**
> he/she was watching his/her favourite programme

ii)   **stare** + **per** + *infinitive* corresponds to the English 'to be about to ...':

> **stavamo per telefonarti quando sei arrivato**
> we were about to ring you up when you arrived

Note: the imperfect is sometimes used in colloquial Italian to replace the present or past conditional:

> **desidera, signora? - volevo** (*instead of* **vorrei**) **del prosciutto**
> can I help you, madam? - I would like (was wanting) some ham

> **dovevi dirmelo subito** (*instead of* **avresti dovuto dirmelo**)
> you should have told me immediately

> **era meglio se me lo dicevi prima** (*instead of* **se me lo avessi detto**)
> it would have been better if you had told me before

d)   The imperfect is also used to render the English pluperfect when an action which started in the past was still continuing at a given time (see also pp 127-8):

> **studiavo l'inglese da due anni**
> I had been studying English for two years

non fumava da più di un mese
he/she had not been smoking for more than a month

3. Present perfect and past historic

(referred to as the PASSATO PROSSIMO and the PASSATO REMOTO in the conjugation tables, pp 169-88)

The use of the present perfect (**passato prossimo**) and the past historic (**passato remoto**) varies geographically in Italy.

a) In the more central parts of Italy a distinction is made between the two. The present perfect is used to refer to a past action which is somehow related to the present. The past historic is used to refer to a completed action in the past:

present perfect

l'ho aspettato tutto il giorno
I've waited for him all day

hai già mangiato?
have you eaten yet?

l'ho visto ieri
I saw him yesterday

past historic

Dante nacque nel 1265
Dante was born in 1265

i Rossi rimasero in Germania per cinque anni
the Rossis remained in Germany for five years

The past historic is used as a narrative tense (but note that, unlike French, it is also a conversational tense in Italian).

b) In the North of Italy the present perfect is also used to refer to a completely past action, while in the South the past historic is sometimes used to refer to actions related to the present:

North **te l'ho dato martedì**
South **te lo diedi martedì**
I gave it to you on Tuesday

North **ieri siamo andati al parco e ho perso il portafoglio**
South **ieri andammo al parco e persi il portafoglio**
yesterday we went to the park and I lost my purse

4. Present perfect/past historic and imperfect compared

In English, the simple past (did, went, prepared etc) is used to describe both single and repeated actions in the past.

In Italian the *present perfect/past historic* describe *single* actions that happened (or started to happen) in a well defined space of time in the past:

l'Italia è diventata una repubblica nel 1947
Italy became a republic in 1947

sono stata a Venezia due anni fa
I went to Venice two years ago

i fuochi artificiali durarono dalle nove a mezzanotte
the fireworks lasted from nine o'clock till midnight

durante la siccità l'acqua venne razionata
during the drought water was rationed

Repeated, habitual or background actions, which are referred to vaguely, with no clear restrictions on their duration and no mention of their beginning and end are expressed by the *imperfect* (they are sometimes signalled by 'used to' or 'I was ... -ing'). Thus 'I went' should be translated 'andavo' or 'sono andato/andai' depending on the nature of the action:

oggi la lezione di guida è durata due ore (*today only*)
present perfect
today the driving lesson lasted two hours

la lezione di guida durava un'ora (*normally*)
imperfect
the driving lesson lasted one hour

durante l'inverno è stato malato (*only that winter*)
present perfect
he was ill throughout the winter

durante l'inverno era sempre malato (*usually*)
imperfect
he was always ill during the winter

che cosa fece quando lo arrestarono?
past historic
what did he do when they arrested him?

che cosa faceva quando lo arrestarono?
imperfect
what was he doing when they arrested him?

5.   Pluperfect

This compound tense is used to express what someone had done/had been doing or something that had happened or had been happening. It can be used independently or in connection with a perfect or a past historic to express an action which happened previously:

non aveva mai fatto la permanente
she had never had her hair permed

gliel'avevo già detto migliaia di volte!
I had already told him a thousand times!

stava male perché aveva bevuto troppo
he/she wasn't well because he/she had drunk too much

non potè dirglielo perché era già partita
he/she could not tell her because she had already left

Note: adverbs like **mai, già, prima, non ancora, dopo che, appena, quando, perché, siccome** often accompany the pluperfect, stressing the fact that one action happened before the other.

6.   Past anterior

This tense is used instead of the pluperfect to express an action that preceded another action in the past when the main verb is in the past historic. It is always introduced by **dopo che** (after), **appena** (as soon as) or **quando** (when):

dopo che furono entrati tutti, chiuse la porta
after everybody had come in, he/she closed the door

appena furono arrivati, gli consegnarono il pacco
as soon as they had arrived, they gave him the parcel

quando ebbe sentito lo sparo, telefonò alla polizia
when he/she heard the shot, he/she rang the police

7.   Future

a)   This tense is used to express what someone will do or will be doing or something that will happen or will be happening:

il volo BA615 per Genova partirà con un'ora di ritardo
BA flight 615 to Genoa will leave one hour late

vi telefoneremo giovedì
we'll call you on Thursday

Note: for the use of the present instead of the future, see p 124

b)   The future is also used to express probability in sentences like:

>   **quanti anni avrà? - non so, ne avrà una trentina**
>   how old do you think he/she is? - I don't know, maybe thirty

>   **che ore saranno?**
>   what time could it be?

>   **guadagnerà al massimo un milione e mezzo al mese**
>   he/she can't possibly earn more than one and a half million lire a
>   month

>   **dove mai sarà Gabriella?**
>   where on earth can Gabriella be?

8.   Future perfect

a)   This compound tense is used to describe what someone will have
done/will have been doing in the future or to describe something
that will have happened in the future:

>   **allora avrò sicuramente finito**
>   I will definitely have finished by then

>   **quando lo avranno aperto al pubblico ci andremo**
>   when they open it to the public, we will go

b)   The future perfect can also express probability in sentences like:

>   **è partito subito: avrà avuto fretta**
>   he left straight away: he must have been in a hurry

>   **non è ancora arrivata: che cosa le sarà successo?**
>   she hasn't arrived yet: what can have happened to her?

9.   Present perfect and past perfect progressive

a)   The present must be used instead of the perfect to describe actions
which started in the past and have continued until the present:

>   **abita qui da tre anni**
>   he/she's been living here for three years

>   **lo aspetta da stamattina**
>   he/she's been waiting for him since this morning

Note:
i)   notice the use of the preposition **da** (from) where English has
'for'

ii)   the sentence **ha abitato qui per tre anni** is also possible, but it
means 'he lived here for three years' (and now he lives
somewhere else)

b)   The imperfect must be used instead of the pluperfect to describe an
action which had started in the past and was still going on at a given
time:

> **quando ti incontrai, studiavi l'italiano da due mesi**
> when I met you, you had been studying Italian for two months

> **aspettava da tre ore quando siamo arrivati**
> he/she had been waiting for three hours when we arrived

Note:
   i)   notice the use of the preposition **da** (from) where English has
        'for'

   ii) a sentence like **aveva studiato l'italiano per due mesi** is also
        possible, but it would mean 'he had studied Italian for two
        months' but was no longer studying it

G. THE SUBJUNCTIVE

The subjunctive in Italian has four tenses: present, imperfect, perfect and pluperfect. For the formation of these tenses see p 103 and pp 107-9.

penso che Mario studi molto
I think Mario studies hard
(present)

penso che abbia studiato molto
I think he studied hard
(perfect)

pensavo che studiasse molto
I thought he studied hard
(imperfect)

pensavo che avesse studiato molto
I thought he had studied hard
(pluperfect)

In Italian, unlike English, the subjunctive is used extensively. It is used in both main and subordinate clauses. In subordinate clauses a choice between the subjunctive and the indicative is often possible. When a formal register is sought, the subjunctive is always to be preferred whereas the indicative may be found in colloquial and regional varieties of Italian. It should also be remembered that the indicative expresses a greater degree of certainty than the subjunctive.

In many of the following examples the use of the indicative would also be possible, but often with a difference in implication. For example:

ho paura che l'ha perso *(indicative)*
I'm afraid that he/she has lost it *(I know for a fact)*

ho paura che l'abbia perso *(subjunctive)*
I'm afraid that he/she has lost it *(that he/she might have lost it)*

era il solo cavallo che poteva vincere *(indicative)*
it was the only horse that could win *(a fact given the circumstances)*

era il solo cavallo che potesse vincere *(subjunctive)*
it was the only horse that could win *(in my opinion)*

Sometimes, however, there is little difference between the use of the indicative and the subjunctive, the latter simply expressing a higher level of formality:

temo che farà freddo domani
temo che faccia freddo domani
I'm afraid it will be cold tomorrow

1. Use of the subjunctive in main clauses

The subjunctive is used in main clauses to express a wish or a doubt:

siate felici!
may you be happy!

che abbia mangiato troppo?
I wonder if I have eaten too much?

It is also used to form the polite form (for **lei/loro**) of the imperative:

vada piano   go slowly

It is also used in exclamations and concessive expressions:

sapessi che divertimento!
if you knew what fun it is/was!

sia ricco o no
be he rich or not

2. Use of the subjunctive in subordinate clauses

The subjunctive can be used after the following:

a)   Verbs of emotion:

essere arrabbiato che	to be angry that
essere contento/scontento che	to be pleased/displeased that
essere felice/infelice che	to be happy/unhappy that
aver paura che	to be afraid that
rammaricarsi che	to regret that
rincrescere che	to regret that
essere sorpreso/stupito che	to be surprised that
stupirsi che	to be surprised that
essere spiacente che	to be sorry that
temere che	to fear that

erano contenti che nevicasse
they were pleased that it snowed

avevano paura che fosse troppo tardi
they were worried that it was too late

b)   Verbs of wishing, willing, allowing and preventing:

augurarsi che	to wish (that)
impedire che	to prevent
lasciare che	to let
permettere che	to allow
preferire che	to prefer
sperare che	to hope
volere che	to want

spero che tu abbia un po' di fortuna
I hope that you will be lucky

si auguravano che l'aereo partisse presto
they wished that the plane would leave soon

Note: in English such verbs are often used in the following types of construction: verb of willing + object + infinitive (eg *I'd like you to listen*); this type of construction is impossible in Italian, where a subjunctive clause has to be used:

permise che giocassero a tennis sul suo prato
he/she allowed them to play tennis on his/her lawn

vorrebbe che tu lo andassi a trovare più spesso
he/she would like you to go and visit him more often

c) Impersonal constructions (expressing necessity, possibility, doubt, denial, preference):

basta che	it is enough (that)
è bene/male che	it is a good/bad thing that
bisogna che	it is necessary (that), ... must
conviene che	one had better
è facile/difficile che	it is easy/difficult for
	it is likely/unlikely that
è meglio/peggio che	it is better/worse that
è naturale che	it is natural that
è necessario che	it is necessary that
è un peccato che	it is a pity (that)
è possibile/impossibile che	it is possible/impossible that
è preferibile che	it is preferable (that)
è probabile/improbabile che	it is likely/unlikely that
sembra che	it seems (that)
è strano che	it is odd that
è utile/inutile che	it is useful/useless that
vale la pena che	it is worth

è inutile che tu ti preoccupi per quell'esame
it is pointless for you to worry about the exam

converrà che usciamo presto per trovare un posteggio
we had better leave early to find a parking space

Note: in English, such expressions are also used in the following type of construction: impersonal expression + (for) + object + infinitive. A subjunctive clause must be used in Italian to convey the same meaning:

è importante che tu abbia successo
it's important for you to succeed

vale la pena che stiri i tuoi calzoni?
is it worth my ironing your trousers?

d) Some verbs of knowledge, perception and affirmation, in particular in the negative and interrogative:

(non) sapere se	(not) to know whether
(non) credere che	(not) to believe, think that
(non) vedere come	(not) to see how
(non) affermare che	(not) to assert that
(non) dire che	(not) to say that

non so se sia già ora di cena
I don't know whether it's dinner time yet

non vedo come possa trovarlo attraente
I don't see how she can find him attractive

credi che l'autobus sia già passato?
do you think the bus has already gone?

e) Verbs of thought, doubt and denial:

pensare che	to think that
parere/sembrare che	to seem that
dubitare che	to doubt that
negare che	to deny that

dubito che si ricordi di passare in tintoria
I don't think he'll remember to go to the drycleaner's

pensavo che fossero partiti per le vacanze
I thought they had left for their holidays

f) Verbs of asking followed by indirect questions:

chiedere se	to ask whether
domandare se	to ask whether

domandò se lì facesse freddo
he/she asked if it was cold there

mi chiedo se siano soldi ben spesi
I ask myself whether it is money well spent

g) **attendere che/aspettare che** (to wait until, to wait for someone to do something):

aspettiamo che sia di buon umore
let's wait until he/she is in a good mood

h) Some subordinating conjunctions and subordinating expressions (note that the following are ALWAYS followed by the subjunctive):

affinché/perché	so that
benché/sebbene/quantunque	(al)though

nonostante che	in spite of
purché/a patto che/a condizione che	provided that
nel caso che/qualora/caso mai	in case
come se	as if
senza che	without
di modo che/in maniera che	so that
a meno che (non)...	unless
prima che (non)...	before
per paura che (non)...	for fear that

Note: in the last three expressions **non** does not have a negative meaning, and is not translated in English.

telefono perché tu sappia che l'aereo è in ritardo
I'm ringing to let you know that the plane is late

sebbene sia passato un anno ne parla sempre
although a year has gone by he/she still talks about it all the time

ecco il mio numero, qualora le servisse
here's my number in case you need it

la salutò come se la conoscesse
he/she greeted her as if he/she knew her

laverò le lenzuola domani, a meno che non cambi il tempo
I'll wash the sheets tomorrow unless the weather changes

voglio vedere dei miglioramenti prima che finisca il trimestre
I want to see some improvements before the term is over

camminiamo in punta dei piedi in modo che non ci sentano
let's go on tiptoe so that they don't hear us

Note: **di modo che/in maniera che** (so that) take the indicative and not the subjunctive when used to express a result as opposed to a purpose:

fece rumore, di modo che lo sentirono
he made a noise, and so they heard him

Note: **perché** takes the indicative when it means 'because'

i) Indefinite adjectives and pronouns introducing clauses:

chiunque	**qualunque**
whoever	whichever
qualsiasi	**qualunque cosa**
whichever	whatever

chiunque lo pensi sbaglia
whoever thinks that is wrong

qualsiasi cosa tu dica avrà gran peso
whatever you say will carry great weight

j) The second term of comparison in comparative clauses:

> **è più serena di quanto sperassi**
> she is calmer than I had hoped

k) A superlative of an adjective or the words **primo** (first), **ultimo** (last), **solo/unico** (only) followed by a relative clause:

> **è il ragazzo più testardo che conosca**
> he is the most stubborn boy I know

l) Negative or indefinite pronouns or adjectives like **nessuno** (no one, no), **niente/nulla** (nothing), **qualcuno** (somebody) in dependent relative clauses:

> **non c'è niente che mi commuova tanto**
> there is nothing that moves me so much

> **non c'è nessuna probabilità che siano liberati**
> there is no chance that they will be freed

> **cercano qualcuno che faccia da interprete**
> they are looking for somebody to act as interpreter

m) **che** when it introduces subordinate clauses which precede the main clause:

> **che sia abile lo so già**
> that he/she is capable I already know

n) For the use of the subjunctive in if-clauses see p 143.

3. Restrictions on the use of the subjunctive

If the subject of the main clause and that of the subordinate clause are the same, then the subjunctive is replaced by a construction with the infinitive. The infinitive can be introduced by **di**, by no preposition at all or by **a**:

a) **di** + infinitive replaces the subjunctive after:

   i)   verbs of emotion:

> **furono contenti di partire**   **sei felice di rivederla?**
> they were happy to leave   are you happy to see her again?

> **avevo paura di essere in ritardo**
> I was worried that I was late/about being late

ii) some verbs of wishing, willing, allowing:

spero di finire questo lavoro presto
I hope to finish this job soon

si augurarono di non rivederlo più
they wished never to see him again

iii) verbs of knowledge, perception and affirmation:

non credo di pretendere troppo
I don't think that I'm expecting too much

non pensavo di essere l'unico
I didn't think I was the only one

iv) verbs of thought, doubt and denial:

pensate di passare inosservati?
do you think you can go unnoticed?

negavano di essere terroristi
they denied that they were terrorists

v) **attendere, aspettare**:

attendevano di passare la dogana
they were waiting to go through Customs

vi) some conjunctions and subordinating expressions:

si pettinò prima di uscire
he/she combed his/her hair before going out

spensero la luce per paura di esser visti
they turned the light off for fear of being seen

voleva dimagrire per mettersi il due pezzi
she wanted to lose weight to wear a bikini

parlò senza balbettare
he/she spoke without stuttering

b) The infinitive without any linking preposition replaces the subjunctive after:

i) **bisogna, basta** and most impersonal verbs and expressions:

basta rinunciare alla carne per sentirsi meglio
all you have to do is give up meat to feel better

è inutile lamentarsi adesso

it is no use complaining now

ii) some verbs of wishing, willing, allowing:

preferisco nuotare all'alba
I prefer to swim at dawn

volevano concludere l'affare
they wanted to clinch the deal

iii) **se** introducing indirect questions:

non sapevo se ridere o piangere
I didn't know whether to laugh or cry

c) The infinitive is preceded by the preposition **a** after **primo** (first), **ultimo** (last), **solo/unico** (only):

è stata la prima ad andarsene
she was the first to leave

4. Sequence of tenses with the subjunctive

Two considerations determine which tense of the subjunctive is used in subordinate clauses. These are:

* the tense used in the main clause
* the time relationship between the main clause and the subordinate clause, that is whether the subordinate clause describes an action which is contemporary with the action in the main clause, which follows the action in the main clause or which is previous to the action in the main clause.

a) When the verb in the main clause is in the present or future indicative, the tense in the subordinate clause will be:

i) the present subjunctive to describe a contemporary or a following action:

penso che oggi studino in biblioteca
I think they are studying in the library today

spero che la prossima settimana tu stia meglio
I hope that you feel better next week

farò finta che tu non sia qui
I'll pretend you're not here

ii) the perfect subjunctive to describe a previous action:

la polizia cerca testimoni che abbiano notato la macchina
the police are looking for witnesses who noticed the car

chiederà come siano riusciti a spendere tanto
he/she will ask how they managed to spend so much

b) When the verb of the main clause is in the imperfect indicative, past historic, perfect or pluperfect, the tense used in the subordinate clause will be:

i) the imperfect subjunctive to describe a contemporary action:

pensavo che fossero stanchi per il viaggio
I thought that they were tired on account of the journey

gli sembrò che il clima fosse ideale
it seemed to him that the climate was ideal

hanno creduto che venisse da lontano
they thought that he/she came from far away

avevano cercato una casa che avesse un bel giardino
they had looked for a house that had a nice garden

ii) the pluperfect subjunctive to describe a previous action:

cercavano qualcuno che avesse lavorato in quella fabbrica
they were looking for someone who had worked in that factory

chiese se le avessero già spedito il pacco
she asked whether they had already sent the parcel to her

hanno sbagliato strada nonostante avessero ricevuto istruzioni dettagliate
they took the wrong road in spite of having received detailed instructions

non era riuscito a scoprire se avessero telefonato o no
he couldn't ascertain whether they had phoned or not

iii) to describe a following action the past conditional is used (see pp 141-2 Conditional):

speravo che avebbero trovato un lavoro
I hoped that they would find a job

H. THE CONDITIONAL

The conditional describes an action that could happen (or might have happened) under certain conditions. It has two tenses: present and past. For the forms of the conditional see p 102.

1. Use of the present conditional

a) To describe an action that could take place in the present or the future:

> **oggi risolverei quel problema in modo diverso**
> today I would solve the problem in a different way

b) To express a wish or desire:

> **vorrei un caffè**
> I would like a coffee

> **potrei cucinare la torta domani?**
> could I bake the cake tomorrow?

c) To express a doubt concerning a present or future action:

> **che cosa dovrei fare?**
> what should I do?

d) To express an action, situation or occurrence which would be possible on certain conditions:

> **se avessi tempo, *andrei* volentieri al cinema**
> if I had the time, I would gladly go to the cinema

e) To express a certainty:

> **non farei mai una cosa simile!**
> I would never do such a thing!

f) To express discreetly a personal opinion:

> **penso che sarebbe una buona idea**
> I think this would be a good idea

g) With reported speech:

> **dice che accetterebbe la vostra proposta**
> he/she says he/she would accept your proposal

advantage card

1 point = 1 penny to spend on treats in store and online

*T & Cs apply, see application form in store for details.

MIX
Paper from
responsible sources
FSC® C041232

Collect 4 points for every

let's feel good

Boots UK Limited
PEEBLES - 646
(01721) 720613

1/05/2014   12:12
Served by: Cheryl   £

Germlds Crm 55g   5.35

TOTAL TO PAY   **5.35**
CASH   10.00
CHANGE   4.65

let's feel good

PLEASE RETAIN THIS RECEIPT SO YOUR
POINTS CAN BE ADJUSTED IF YOU
VISIT ANY UK STORE WITH YOUR
CARD IN THE NEXT 45 DAYS

|||||||||||||||||||||||||||||||||||||

TRANSACTION CODE
6686 89841 59283 54446 87703 98
POINTS VALUE   20

101 1981 0646 133

010199999999991292

h) To express the possibility that something is happening in the present:

> **secondo questo articolo gli ostaggi sarebbero a Beirut**
> according to this article the hostages are in Beirut

2. Use of the past conditional

a) To describe an action that might have taken place in the past:

> **avrei potuto cucinare la torta ieri sera**
> I could have baked the cake yesterday evening

b) To express an unfulfilled wish or desire referring to the past:

> **avrei voluto un caffè**
> I would have liked a coffee

c) To express doubt concerning a past action:

> **che cosa avrei dovuto fare?**
> what should I have done?

d) To express a past action, situation or occurrence which would have been possible on certain conditions:

> **avrebbe accettato la tua proposta se avessi cancellato il paragrafo 3**
> he/she would have accepted your proposal if you had dropped clause 3

e) To express a sense of surprise or disbelief about a past action:

> **non avrei mai fatto una cosa simile!**
> I would never have done such a thing!

f) To express discreetly a personal opinion about a past action:

> **penso che sarebbe stata una buona idea**
> I think it would have been a good idea

g) With reported speech:

> **disse che avrebbe accettato la tua proposta**
> he/she said he/she would accept your proposal

Note: in this case Italian, unlike English, MUST use the past conditional

h) To express the possibility that something was happening in the past:

> **secondo quell'articolo gli ostaggi sarebbero stati a Beirut**
> according to that article the hostages were in Beirut

Note:

i) when 'would' implies 'resolve', it is expressed by **volere**:

> **non mi volle ascoltare**
> he/she would not listen to me

ii) when 'would' suggests repeated action, it is conveyed by the imperfect indicative:

> **d'estate innaffiava il giardino ogni sera**
> in summer he/she would water the garden every evening

iii) when 'should' means 'ought to', it is expressed by **dovere**:

> **dovresti fare più sport**
> you should do more sport

3. Sequence of tenses with the conditional

a) When the verb in the main clause is in the present (or future) indicative, the tense used in the subordinate clause will be:

i) the present conditional to describe a contemporary or a following action:

> **penso che adesso verrebbero volentieri**
> I think that they would be pleased to come now

> **credo che Carlo ci potrebbe andare domani**
> I think Carlo could go there tomorrow

ii) the past conditional to describe a previous action:

> **penso che avrebbe dovuto farlo**
> I think he/she should have done it

b) When the verb in the main clause is in the imperfect indicative, past historic, perfect or pluperfect, the tense used in the subordinate clause will be:

i) the imperfect subjunctive to describe a contemporary action (see p 139)

ii) the pluperfect subjunctive to describe a previous action (see p 139)

iii) the past conditional to describe a following action:

pensavo che lo avresti finito in tempo
I thought you would finish it in time

4. Use of tenses in if-clauses

a) If the main clause refers to the present or to the future, the verb in the main clause uses the present conditional and the verb in the conditional clause (if-clause) uses:

i) the imperfect subjunctive, if the action it expresses is contemporary with the action in the main clause:

se lo sapessi te lo direi
I would tell you if I knew

se non guardassi la TV avresti tempo per leggere
if you didn't watch TV you would have time to read

ii) the pluperfect subjunctive, if the action it expresses is previous to the action in the main clause:

se avessi studiato di più, ora passeresti l'esame
if you had studied more, you would pass the exam

se ieri non avessi guardato la TV, ora non saprei tutto sull'argomento
if I hadn't watched TV yesterday, I wouldn't now know all there is to know on this subject

b) If the main clause refers to the past, the verb in the main clause is in the past conditional and the verb in the 'if' clause uses the pluperfect subjunctive:

se lo avessi saputo te lo avrei detto
I would have told you if I had known

se fosse stato più giovane avrebbe dormito in tenda
if he had been younger he would have slept in the tent

Note: in Italian never use the conditional in a clause with **se** meaning 'if'

I. THE IMPERATIVE

1. Definition

The imperative is used to give commands, or polite instructions, or to make requests or suggestions. These can be positive ('do!') or negative ('don't!') and they can refer to the present or to the future:

vieni subito qua!
come here straight away!

non aver paura!
don't be afraid!

la prossima volta chiedete scusa!
next time apologize!

andiamo
let's go

non continuate!
don't go on!

non esca
don't go out

camminate sul marciapiede
keep to the pavement

all'incrocio girate a destra
turn right at the crossroads

2. Forms

a) The forms of the imperative for the **tu** and **voi** forms are identical to those of the present indicative with the exception of the **tu** form of first conjugation (**-are**) verbs:

	-are VERBS	-ere VERBS	-ire VERBS
SING FORM 'TU'	parla	credi	dormi
PLURAL FORM 'VOI'	parlate	credete	dormite

b) To express an imperative in the first person plural (**noi**) and in the polite form (**lei, loro**) the corresponding forms of the present subjunctive are used:

corriamo veloci! (*noi*)
let's run fast!

continui sempre dritto! (*lei*)
carry straight on!

vada pure (*lei*)
by all means go

si accomodino, prego (*loro*)
please be seated

abbiano pazienza (*loro*)
be patient

3. Irregular imperatives (*tu* and *voi* forms)

The two auxiliary verbs (**essere** and **avere**) use the following forms:

	SING	PLURAL	
essere	**sii**	**siate**	be
avere	**abbi**	**abbiate**	have

The following common verbs have some irregular forms which are different from the present indicative;

	SING	PLURAL	
andare	**va'**	**andate**	go
dare	**da'**	**date**	give
dire	**di'**	**dite**	say
fare	**fa'**	**fate**	do, make
sapere	**sappi**	**sappiate**	you must know
stare	**sta'**	**state**	be

4. Negative commands

In negative commands **non** precedes the affirmative forms of the verb. In the **tu** form, however, **non** is followed by the infinitive.

2ND PERSON SING	2ND PERSON PLURAL	
non mangiare	**non mangiate**	do not eat
non prendere	**non prendete**	do not take
non finire	**non finite**	do not finish

2ND PERSON SING POLITE	2ND PERSON PLURAL POLITE	
non mangi (*lei*)	**non mangino** (*loro*)	do not eat
	non mangiate (*voi*)	

Note: for a note on the use of **voi** as the plural polite form see p 68

1ST PERSON PLURAL	
non mangiamo	let's not eat

5. The imperative with object pronouns (excluding the polite form)

In positive commands, object pronouns and **ci** (**vi**) and **ne** (see pp 73-4), come after the verb and is attached to it.

credimi!
believe me (*sing 'you' form*)

mandatele un assegno
send her a cheque (*plural 'you' form*)

spiegale di che si tratta
explain to her what it is about (*sing 'you' form*)

scriviamogli subito
let's write to him straight away

andateci voi!
you go there!

Note:

i) **loro** comes after the verb but is written separately:

prendi loro un gelato
get them an ice cream

ii) after the five imperatives **va'**, **da'**, **di'**, **fa'**, **sta'**, pronouns, with the exception of **gli**, double their initial consonant:

dimmi la verità   **stalle vicino**
tell me the truth   stay close to her

But: **fagli compagnia**
keep him company

iii) with a negative command the object pronouns can either follow the verb or be placed between **non** and the verb:

non raccontarmi storie
non mi raccontare storie
don't tell me stories

non pensateci più
non ci pensate più
don't think about it any more

6. Polite form - commands with object pronouns

Object pronouns and **ci** (**vi**) and **ne** always precede polite form commands:

gli offra un caffè	**mi faccia il piacere!**
offer him/them a cup of coffee	do me a favour!
non mi facciano aspettare	
don't keep me waiting	

Note: **loro** however follows the verb:

dica loro di prenotare un tavolo
tell them to book a table

7. Imperative of reflexive verbs

The position of the reflexive pronouns of reflexive verbs is the same as that of object pronouns:

alzati (*tu*)	**pettinatevi**
get up	comb your hair
non fidatevi di lui	**fermiamoci qua**
don't trust him	let's stop here
si alzi (*lei*)	
get up	

8. Alternatives to the imperative

The infinitive is often used instead of the imperative in written instructions (including recipes and knitting patterns):

non fumare	**non sostare**
no smoking	no stopping
calare dieci maglie	**non ingombrare le uscite**
decrease ten stitches	do not block the exits

J. THE INFINITIVE

1. Definition and forms

The infinitive is the basic form of the verb. It is recognized by its ending, which is found in three forms: **-are** for the first conjugation, **-ere** for the second and **-ire** for the third:

parlare	**credere**	**sentire**
to speak	to believe	to hear

Note:

i) the endings **-are**, **-ere**, **-ire** give the verb the meaning 'to ...'. The Italian infinitive will, however, often be translated by a verb form ending in '-ing' (see p 149).

ii) a few common verbs have irregular infinitives, among them:

tradurre	**produrre**	**condurre**	**porre**
to translate	to produce	to lead	to put

imporre	**proporre**	**comporre**
to impose	to propose	to compose

2. Tenses

The infinitive has two tenses: the present infinitive and the past infinitive. The past infinitive is formed by adding the past participle of the verb to the infinitive of the appropriate auxiliary (see pp 107-14):

PRESENT	PAST
amare	**aver(e) amato**
to love	to have loved
arrivare	**esser(e) arrivato**
to arrive	to have arrived
alzarsi	**essersi alzato**
to get up	to have got up

Note: the final **-e** of **avere** and **essere** can be omitted.

3. Uses of the infinitive

a) *After a preposition*

The infinitive can be used after some prepositions (**prima di, dopo, senza, al fine di, invece di, tra, con, per,** etc):

prima di protestare before complaining	**dopo aver mangiato** after eating
invece di affrettarsi instead of hurrying	**senza pettinarsi** without combing one's hair
per sentirsi bene in order to feel well	

Note: **dopo** is always followed by the past infinit⁻ie

b) *After a verb*

There are three main constructions when a verb is followed by an infinitive:

with no linking preposition
with the linking preposition **a**
with the linking preposition **di**

(For lists of the main verbs in each category see pp 189-96)

i) verbs followed by the infinitive with no linking preposition

Many of these verbs belong to the following groups:

★ modal verbs:

dovere	must, to have to
potere	can, to be able to
volere	will, to want to

vuoi fare una doccia?
do you want to have a shower?

devo lavare i piatti
I have to do the dishes

★ verbs of seeing, hearing:

vedere	**guardare**	**sentire**	**ascoltare**
to see	to watch	to hear	to listen to

di domenica ascoltavo le campane suonare
on Sundays I listened to the bells ringing

mi hai guardata ballare?
did you watch me dance?

★ most impersonal verbs:

conviene accettare quell'offerta
it's better to accept that offer

bisogna pagare
you have to pay

occorre pensarci sopra
it's necessary to think it over

★ impersonal expressions with **essere**:

è sempre piacevole parlare con te
it's always pleasant to talk with you

è difficile trovarlo a casa
it's difficult to find him at home

★ verbs of liking and disliking, eg:

amare	to love, to be fond of
adorare	to adore, to love
detestare	to hate
piacere	to like
preferire	to prefer

amo ascoltare musica classica
I'm fond of listening to classical music

preferiscono viaggiare di notte
they prefer travelling by night

ii) verbs with the linking preposition **a**

Many of these verbs belong to the following groups:

★ verbs of motion:

andare	to go
venire	to come
entrare	to go/come in
uscire	to go/come out
salire	to go/come up
scendere	to go/come down

salga a vedere come sta
go up and see how he/she is

vieni a discutere questo problema da me
come and discuss this problem at my place

va' a comprare il giornale
go and buy a newspaper

Note: in English these verbs may be linked by 'and' to the verb that follows; 'and' is not expressed in Italian

★ verbs of beginning, continuing, preparing:

cominciare	**iniziare**	**continuare**	**prepararsi**
to begin	to begin	to continue	to get ready

all'alba gli uccelli cominciarono a cantare
at dawn the birds began to sing

si preparavano a suonare
they were getting ready to play

★ verbs of teaching and learning:

apprendere	**imparare**	**insegnare**
to learn	to learn	to teach

imparò a cavalcare in poche lezioni
he/she learned to ride in a few lessons

ci insegnò a parlare italiano
he/she taught us to speak Italian

★ verbs of compulsion:

furono costretti a consegnare il denaro
they were forced to hand over the money

★ the expressions **far bene, far male** etc:

hai fatto bene a vendere la casa
you were right to sell your house

★ **essere** followed by a numeral or by **solo, ultimo**:

furono i primi a scusarsi
they were the first to apologize

sei il solo a non sentire la sveglia
you are the only one who can't hear the alarm clock

iii) verbs with the linking preposition **di**

These include the majority of Italian verbs. Many belong to the following groups:

★ verbs of hope, belief, knowledge:

credo di sbagliare
I believe I am wrong

speravano di tornare in Inghilterra
they hoped to go back to England

sapeva di essere in ritardo
he/she knew he/she was late

★ verbs of commanding:

ordinarono di cessare il fuoco
they ordered a ceasefire

★ verbs of saying, asking:

domandarono di essere svegliati alle sei
they asked to be woken up at six

★ verbs of doubt, uncertainty:

dubito di avere abbastanza tempo
I doubt I'll have enough time

★ verbs of surprise, fear, emotion:

si stupì di vedere un cervo vicino alla strada
he/she was surprised to see a deer close to the road

★ verbs of trying:

cerca di non macchiare la tovaglia
try not to stain the tablecloth

ci sforzeremo di finire questo lavoro in tempo
we'll try to finish this job on time

Note: the verbs **astenersi** (to abstain from) and **contenersi** (to refrain from) are followed by the linking preposition **da**:

durante il giorno si astengono dal mangiare e dal bere
they abstain from eating and drinking during the day

c) *After an adjective*

There are three main constructions when an adjective is followed by an infinitive:

with the linking preposition **a**
with the linking preposition **di**
with the linking preposition **da**

i)   some common adjectives with the linking preposition **a**:

abituato	used
adatto	suitable
autorizzato	authorized, licensed
contrario	against, opposed
deciso	determined
disposto	willing
inutile	useless
lento	slow
pronto	ready
utile	useful

sono pronta a partire
I'm ready to leave

è deciso a vincere l'incontro
he's determined to win the match

quel negozio è autorizzato a vendere vini e liquori
that shop is licensed to sell wines and spirits

ii)   some common adjectives with the linking preposition **di**:

ansioso	anxious
bramoso	eager
certo	certain
contento	happy
curioso	curious
degno	worthy
desideroso	keen
felice	happy, glad
impaziente	impatient
indegno	unworthy
infelice	unhappy
lieto	happy
scontento	dissatisfied
sicuro	certain
stanco	tired

felice di conoscerla!
pleased to meet you!

erano impazienti di chiarire l'equivoco
they were anxious to clear up the misunderstanding

siamo desiderosi di ricevere vostre notizie
we are keen to hear your news

iii) some common adjectives with the linking preposition **da**:

bello	beautiful
buffo	funny
differente	different
difficile	difficult
divertente	amusing
facile	easy
gradevole	pleasant
sgradevole	unpleasant

è facile da usare
it's easy to use

Pietro è difficile da capire
Pietro is difficult to understand

Note: in constructions with **essere**, adjectives can also be followed by **da** + infinitive to convey the idea of 'to a very high degree':

è simpatico da morire
he's extremely pleasant

d) *After a noun*

There are three possible constructions:

with **da**
with **di**
with **per**

i) **da** is used in the majority of cases and conveys the idea of something to be done:

hanno una casa da vendere
they have a house for sale

ci ha mostrato la strada da seguire
he/she showed us the road to follow

ci sono solo tre libri da leggere per questo corso
there are only three books to read for this course

ii) **di** is used to define something more closely:

non è il momento di disturbarlo
now is not the time to disturb him

avevano piacere di trovarsi ogni tanto
they were happy to meet from time to time

iii) **per** is used to express aim or purpose:

i soldi per andare all'estero
the money to go abroad

Gabrio sta risparmiando per comprarsi il motorino
Gabrio's saving up to buy a moped

e) *fare* + **infinitive**

fare is followed by an infinitive without any linking preposition to express the idea of 'making someone do something' or 'having something done':

fa' pulire quel tappeto
have that carpet cleaned

mi ha fatto aspettare per delle ore!
he/she kept me waiting for hours!

farò prenotare una cuccetta
I'll book a sleeper

Note: when both verbs (**fare** and the following infinitive) have an object in English, the object of **fare** becomes indirect in Italian:

fecero cambiare le lenzuola alla cameriera
they got the chambermaid to change the sheets

f) *stare per* + **infinitive**

This construction expresses 'to be about to', 'to be on the point of':

stavo per uscire quando si è messo a piovere
I was about to go out when it started to rain

stanno per trasmettere la partita
they are about to broadcast the match

K. PARTICIPLES

1. The present participle

a) *Formation*

The present participle is formed by adding the endings **-ante** (1st conjugation) or **-ente** (2nd and 3rd conjugations) to the stem of the verb. The plural is formed by replacing **-e** with **-i**:

parlante/i	**credente/i**	**udente/i**
speaking	believing	hearing

b) *Use as a verb*

The present participle is used less frequently in Italian than in English. English present participles are often conveyed by the gerund (see p 160) or by the infinitive (see p 149). The following present participles are commonly used with a verbal function:

attestante	testifying	**godente**	enjoying
comandante	commanding	**indicante**	indicating
concernente	concerning	**manifestante**	revealing
contenente	containing	**proveniente**	deriving
eccedente	exceeding	**rappresentante**	representing
formante	forming		

un camion proveniente da Trieste
a lorry coming from Trieste

un certificato attestante la sua frequenza alle lezioni
a certificate testifying his/her class attendance

due valigie contenenti i loro regali di nozze
two suitcases containing their wedding presents

Note:
i) **comandante** and **rappresentante** are, however, mainly used as nouns:

il comandante in capo   **il rappresentante esclusivo**
the commander-in-chief   the sole agent

ii) the present participle must be used with caution. When in doubt it is better to use a relative clause:

un uccello che canta
a bird singing

c) *Use as an adjective or as a noun*

Present participles are most frequently used as adjectives:

frustrante	(*adjective*)	frustrating
crescente	(*adjective*)	growing

Note: the formation of a few participles is irregular:

nutriente	(*adjective*)	nourishing
ubbidiente	(*adjective*)	obedient
seguente	(*adjective*)	following

Some present participles can be both a noun and an adjective:

corrente	(*noun*)	stream
corrente	(*adjective*)	running
docente	(*noun*)	teacher
docente	(*adjective*)	teaching

Note: some present participles originate from verbs which are no longer used in contemporary Italian:

mittente	(*noun*)	sender
abbiente	(*adjective*)	well-off

2. The past participle

a) *Formation*

The past participle is formed by adding the endings below to the stem of the verb. The feminine and plural endings of the past participle are the same as adjective endings:

1st conjugation	-ato/a/i/e
2nd conjugation	-uto/a/i/e
3rd conjugation	-ito/a/i/e

mangiato/a/i/e	**veduto/a/i/e**	**partito/a/i/e**

b) *Use*

The past participle is used in compound tenses and in the passive:

Mario ha scritto una poesia
Mario wrote a poem

quell'edificio è stato costruito in tre giorni
that building was built in three days

3. Agreement of the past participle

a) When the auxiliary is **essere**, the past participle agrees with the subject:

> **Cesare è tornato in Italia**
> Cesare went back to Italy

> **Simona è partita per Napoli**
> Simona has left for Naples

> **i regali sono stati divisi equamente**
> the presents were divided equally

> **dove sono andate quelle studentesse?**
> where have those (women) students gone?

b) When the auxiliary is **avere** and the direct object is not expressed, the past participle does not agree with the subject:

> **Donatella ha insegnato qui per due anni**
> Donatella has taught here for two years

c) When the auxiliary is **avere** and the direct object is expressed *after* the participle, no agreement takes place:

> **Michela ha comprato tre libri**
> Michela bought three books

d) When the auxiliary is **avere** and the direct object is expressed *before* the participle, agreement is optional (but the second form is more common):

> **i libri che Nadia ha comprati**
> **i libri che Nadia ha comprato**
> the books Nadia bought

e) When the auxiliary is **avere**, and the direct object is one of the personal pronouns **lo**, **la**, **li**, **le** and precedes the verb, the past participle agrees with the direct object:

> **lo ha comprato ieri**   (il libro)
> he/she bought it yesterday   (the book)

> **le ha comprate oggi**   (le banane)
> he/she bought them today   (the bananas)

f) When the auxiliary is **avere**, and the direct object is one of the pronouns **mi, ti, ci, vi** and **ne** (partitive) and precedes the verb, agreement with the direct object is optional:

> **mi dispiace, Silvia, se ti ho disturbato**
> **mi dispiace, Silvia, se ti ho disturbata**
> I'm sorry if I bothered you, Silvia

> **ha mangiato della pasta:**   **ne ha mangiata**
> he/she ate some pasta: **ne ha mangiato**
>   he/she ate some of it

Note: it there is another qualifying word in the same sentence which shows agreement then the past participle *must* also agree:

> **ne ha mangiata troppa!**   he/she ate too much (of it)!

g) With reflexive verbs the past participle can agree with either the subject or the object:

> **Lucia si è lavata le mani**
> **Lucia si è lavate le mani**
> Lucia washed her hands

h) When used as an adjective, the past participle always agrees:

> **una camicia stirata**   **un animale ammalato**
> an ironed shirt   a sick animal

> **delle stampate colorate**   **tre piatti rotti**
> some coloured prints   three broken plates

L.   THE GERUND

1.   The present gerund

a)   *Forms*

The present gerund is formed by adding to the stem of each conjugation the endings **-ando** (-are verbs) or **-endo** (-ere and -ire verbs):

parlando	**credendo**	**aprendo**
speaking	believing	opening

The present gerund is invariable and there are no irregular forms.

b)   *Use*

The present gerund is used to express the mode of an action (ie it has an adverbial function). It refers to the same time as the main clause and usually to the same subject:

si fece male cadendo
he hurt himself falling

passeggiando per il parco incontro molti conoscenti
walking in the park I meet many acquaintances

arriverà lì prima prendendo la circonvallazione
you will get there earlier by taking the ring road

sbagliando si impara (*proverb*)
one learns by making mistakes

Note: the gerund is never preceded by a preposition

c)   *Special constructions with the present gerund*

   i)   **stare** + gerund:

   This construction suggests a continuous action:

   sto cucinando
   I'm cooking

   sta mangiandosi il patrimonio
   he/she is eating up his/her legacy

   stava facendo la doccia quando suonò il telefono
   he/she was having a shower when the phone rang

Note: the imperfect is the only past tense with which this construction can be used

ii)   **andare** + gerund:

This suggests repeated, methodical action:

andava raccontando storie incredibili
he/she went around telling incredible tales

2.   The perfect gerund

a)   *Forms*

The perfect gerund is formed with the gerund of the auxiliary **essere** or **avere** as appropriate (see pp 110-14) followed by the past participle of the verb:

avendo amato having loved	**essendo arrivato** having arrived	
essendosi alzato having got up	**essendo stato** having been	**avendo avuto** having had

When the perfect gerund is conjugated with **essere** the past participle, but not the gerund, agrees with the subject.

b)   *Use*

The perfect gerund refers to a time which precedes that of the main clause, but its use is not very common. It usually refers to the same subject:

Gianni, avendo sentito la sirena, scappò
Gianni, having heard the siren, ran away

M. THE PASSIVE

1. Formation

The passive is used with transitive verbs when the subject does not perform the action but is subjected to it, eg:

active: the mayor opened the exhibition
passive: the exhibition was opened by the mayor

Passive tenses are formed with the corresponding tense of the verb **essere** ('to be', as in English) followed by the past participle of the verb:

sono stato invitato
I was invited

a) The past participle must agree with the subject:

quella ragazza è stata licenziata   **gli inquilini sono stati sfrattati**
that girl was dismissed   the tenants have been evicted

le attrici sono state intervistate
the actresses have been interviewed

b) Prepositions with passive verbs:

When the agent or the doer of the action is mentioned, it is preceded by **da** 'by':

active   **Montale ha scritto questa poesia**
Montale wrote this poem

passive   **questa poesia è stata scritta *da* Montale**
this poem was written by Montale

2. Alternative forms

a) In non-compound tenses the verb **venire** can replace **essere**:

oggi la cataratta viene operata col laser
nowadays cataracts are operated on with a laser

il digestivo viene generalmente servito dopo cena
a digestive drink is usually served after dinner

b) The verb **andare** can also be used instead of **dover essere**, meaning 'must be':

le promesse vanno mantenute
promises must be kept

il presidente va servito per primo
the president must be served first

c) *The si passivante*

The passive can also be formed in Italian by placing the pronoun **si** before the third person singular or plural of verbs in the active form:

in quella libreria i libri si vendevano (= erano venduti) a metà prezzo
in that bookshop books used to be sold at half-price

in Italia si vendono (= sono vendute) ancora molte pellicce
in Italy many fur-coats are still sold

col pesce si serve (= è servito) di solito il vino bianco
white wine is usually served with fish

Note: it is easy to confuse the **si** *passivante* with the impersonal **si**, which is only used in the third person singular (see p 121). In the following examples to use the singular **si vede** instead of the plural would be wrong:

oggi si vedono più programmi televisivi che nel passato
nowadays people watch more TV programmes than in the past

da questa finestra si vedono le colline
from this window you can see the hills

For the other uses of **si**, see p 82.

3. **Verbs with indirect objects**

English passive sentences like 'I was taught Italian' cannot be translated literally into Italian, since the Italian verb 'to teach' takes an indirect object. Italian can translate an English passive sentence literally only if the direct object of an active sentence can become the subject of a passive sentence (eg 'I saw *him*' ➡ 'he was seen by me'). One possible translation of 'I was taught Italian' would therefore be **mi è stato insegnato l'italiano**. The subject pronoun has become an indirect object. In reality, however, Italian is much more likely to express this idea without using a passive at all:

mi hanno insegnato l'italiano
they taught me Italian/I was taught Italian

N. MODAL AUXILIARY VERBS

The three modal auxiliary verbs (expressing obligation, probability, ability, wish) are **DOVERE**, **POTERE** and **VOLERE**. They are always followed by an infinitive.

1. DOVERE (conjugation p 175)

    expresses: a) obligation, necessity
                    b) probability
                    c) intention, expectation

a) *Obligation*

> **dovete essere in ufficio per le otto**
> you must be in the office by eight o'clock

> **ho dovuto rispondere subito alla sua lettera**
> I had to answer his/her letter straight away

> **devi lavorare di più**
> you must work harder

> **dovettero portare il loro bagaglio sull'aereo**
> they had to carry their luggage onto the plane

In the conditional, **dovere** can be used to give advice (present conditional) or to express what should have been done (past conditional):

> **dovresti mangiare più verdura**
> you should eat more vegetables

> **avrebbero dovuto evitare quell'incontro**
> they should have avoided that meeting

b) *Probability*

> **dev'essere ancora addormentata**
> she must be still asleep

> **la levata della posta dev'essere a mezzogiorno**
> the mail collection must be at midday

c) *Intention, expectation*

> **devo proprio andare ora**
> I really must go now

> **il treno deve arrivare alle otto**
> the train is due to arrive at eight

2. POTERE (conjugation p 181)

expresses: a) capacity, ability
b) permission
c) possibility

a) *Capacity, ability*

posso mostrartelo subito
I can show it to you straight away

può fare dodici vasche senza fermarsi
he/she can swim twelve lengths without stopping

la mia macchina poteva fare i 150 all'ora
my car could do 150kph

b) *Permission*

posso entrare?   **posso offrirle un caffè?**
may I come in?   may I offer you a cup of coffee?

va bene, puoi guardare i cartoni animati
all right then, you can watch the cartoons

c) *Possibility*

può succedere   **può essere già partito**
it can happen   he may already have left

Note:

i) **potere** also has some idiomatic uses:

non ne posso più
I can't stand it any more

è una persona che può molto
he/she is a very powerful person

ii) with verbs of perception (eg **sentire** to hear/feel, **vedere** to see)
potere is often omitted:

si vedeva l'aurora boreale
you could see the northern lights

iii) in the conditional **potere** can be used to express indignation etc:

potresti salutare quando esci!
you might/could say goodbye when you leave!

avrebbe potuto prestarci dei soldi!
he/she/you could have lent us some money!

3. **VOLERE** (conjugation p 188)

    expresses: a) desire
                    b) wish
                    c) intention

a) *Desire*

    voglio andarmene di qua
    I want to go away from here

    vuol ballare?
    do you want to dance?

b) *Wish*

    vorrei comprare un videoregistratore
    I would like to buy a video recorder

    avrei voluto prenderlo a calci
    I would have liked to kick him

c) *Intention*

    voleva passar la notte alla stazione ferroviaria
    he/she intended to spend the night at the railway station

    cosa vuoi fare da grande?
    what do you want to do when you grow up?

Note:

  i) **volere** has some idiomatic uses:

    vuol bene alla famiglia
    he/she loves his/her family

    ogni mattina sembra che voglia piovere
    every morning it looks as if it might rain

  ii) with **ci**:

    quanto ci vuole da qui alla stazione?
    how long does it take from here to the railway station?

    ci vogliono solo cinque minuti
    it only takes five minutes

    ci vuole un bel coraggio
    it takes some nerve

4. Other modal verbs

Other verbs can have a modal function (ie act as auxiliaries). The most common are **sapere** to know, **osare** to dare:

non oso disturbarlo
I daren't disturb him

sai nuotare?
can you swim?

Note: as a rule **sapere** means 'to know a fact', 'to know how to', while **conoscere** means 'to be acquainted with a person or place':

sa chi era Michelangelo?
do you know who Michelangelo was?

sai leggere i numeri romani?
can you read Roman numerals?

lei non sa chi sono io!
you don't know who you are talking to!

But: **lei non mi conosce**
you don't know me

conosce un bravo idraulico?
do you know a good plumber?

conoscevamo tutti a quel convegno
we knew everybody at that conference

5. Use of the auxiliary with modal verbs

As a rule the modal auxiliary verb takes the auxiliary of the verb it precedes:

sono partito   ➡   **sono dovuto partire**
I've left   I had to leave

non ho dormito   ➡   **non ho potuto dormire**
I didn't sleep   I couldn't sleep

However, when the modal verb precedes an infinitive which takes **essere** as its auxiliary, then the infinitive **avere** can also be used as an alternative:

     non sono potuto andare al mercato
or   **non ho potuto andare al mercato**
     I couldn't go to the market

     è voluto partire a tutti i costi
or   **ha voluto partire a tutti i costi**
     he was determined to go at all costs

erano dovuti ritornare
or   **avevano dovuto ritornare**
they had to go back

Note: for the agreement of past participles see pp 158-9.

6. Use of reflexives with modal verbs

When reflexive infinitives follow modal verbs, the reflexive pronoun can either precede the modal verb or be joined to the infinitive:

ti vuoi sbrigare?
or   **vuoi sbrigarti?**
will you hurry up!

si dovevano lavare con l'acqua fredda
dovevano lavarsi con l'acqua fredda
they had to wash in cold water

Note: in compound tenses the modal verb takes **avere** as its auxiliary when it precedes the reflexive infinitive. However, it takes **essere** as its auxiliary when the reflexive pronoun precedes it:

Gabrio ha dovuto alzarsi presto
Gabrio si è dovuto alzare presto
Gabrio had to get up early

O. CONJUGATION TABLES

The following verbs provide the main patterns of conjugation including the conjugation of some common irregular verbs. They are arranged in alphabetical order.

-are verb	*(see also section A)*	AMARE
-ere verb	*(see also section A)*	TEMERE
-ire verb	*(see also section A)*	SERVIRE
		FINIRE
Reflexive verb	*(see also section D)*	LAVARSI
Auxiliaries	*(see also section C)*	AVERE
		ESSERE
Modal Auxiliary Verbs	*(see also p 164)*	DOVERE
	(see also p 165)	POTERE
	(see also p 166)	VOLERE
Passive	*(see also section M)*	ESSERE AMATO
Common irregular verbs		ANDARE
		DARE
		DIRE
		FARE
		SAPERE
		STARE
		TENERE
		VENIRE

'**Harrap's Italian Verbs**', a fully comprehensive list of Italian verbs and their conjugations, is also available in this series.

AMARE to love

PRESENT	IMPERFECT	FUTURE
1 amo	amavo	amerò
2 ami	amavi	amerai
3 ama	amava	amerà
1 amiamo	amavamo	ameremo
2 amate	amavate	amerete
3 amano	amavano	ameranno

PASSATO REMOTO	PASSATO PROSSIMO	PLUPERFECT
1 amai	ho amato	avevo amato
2 amasti	hai amato	avevi amato
3 amò	ha amato	aveva amato
1 amammo	abbiamo amato	avevamo amato
2 amaste	avete amato	avevate amato
3 amarono	hanno amato	avevano amato

PAST ANTERIOR	FUTURE PERFECT
ebbi amato *etc*	avrò amato *etc*

CONDITIONAL PRESENT	PAST	*IMPERATIVE*
1 amerei	avrei amato	
2 ameresti	avresti amato	
3 amerebbe	avrebbe amato	ama
1 ameremmo	avremmo amato	ami
2 amereste	avreste amato	amiamo
3 amerebbero	avrebbero amato	amate
		amino

SUBJUNCTIVE PRESENT	IMPERFECT	PLUPERFECT
1 ami	amassi	avessi amato
2 ami	amassi	avessi amato
3 ami	amasse	avesse amato
1 amiamo	amassimo	avessimo amato
2 amiate	amaste	aveste amato
3 amino	amassero	avessero amato

PASSATO PROSSIMO	abbia amato *etc*

INFINITIVE PRESENT	*GERUND*	*PAST PARTICIPLE*
amare	amando	amato
PAST		
aver(e) amato		

ANDARE to go

PRESENT	IMPERFECT	FUTURE
1 vado	andavo	andrò
2 vai	andavi	andrai
3 va	andava	andrà
1 andiamo	andavamo	andremo
2 andate	andavate	andrete
3 vanno	andavano	andranno

PASSATO REMOTO	PASSATO PROSSIMO	PLUPERFECT
1 andai	sono andato/a	ero andato/a
2 andasti	sei andato/a	eri andato/a
3 andò	è andato/a	era andato/a
1 andammo	siamo andati/e	eravamo andati/e
2 andaste	siete andati/e	eravate andati/e
3 andarono	sono andati/e	erano andati/e

PAST ANTERIOR		FUTURE PERFECT
fui andato/a etc		sarò andato/a etc

CONDITIONAL		IMPERATIVE
PRESENT	PAST	
1 andrei	sarei andato/a	
2 andresti	saresti andato/a	va/vai/va'
3 andrebbe	sarebbe andato/a	vada
1 andremmo	saremmo andati/e	andiamo
2 andreste	sareste andati/e	andate
3 andrebbero	sarebbero andati/e	vadano

SUBJUNCTIVE		
PRESENT	IMPERFECT	PLUPERFECT
1 vada	andassi	fossi andato/a
2 vada	andassi	fossi andato/a
3 vada	andasse	fosse andato/a
1 andiamo	andassimo	fossimo andati/e
2 andiate	andaste	foste andati/e
3 vadano	andassero	fossero andati/e

PASSATO PROSSIMO		
sia andato/a etc		

INFINITIVE	GERUND	PAST PARTICIPLE
PRESENT	andando	andato/a/i/e
andare		
PAST		
esser(e) andato/a/i/e		

AVERE to have

PRESENT	IMPERFECT	FUTURE
1 ho	avevo	avrò
2 hai	avevi	avrai
3 ha	aveva	avrà
1 abbiamo	avevamo	avremo
2 avete	avevate	avrete
3 hanno	avevano	avranno

PASSATO REMOTO	PASSATO PROSSIMO	PLUPERFECT
1 ebbi	ho avuto	avevo avuto
2 avesti	hai avuto	avevi avuto
3 ebbe	ha avuto	aveva avuto
1 avemmo	abbiamo avuto	avevamo avuto
2 aveste	avete avuto	avevate avuto
3 ebbero	hanno avuto	avevano avuto

PAST ANTERIOR		FUTURE PERFECT
ebbi avuto *etc*		avrò avuto *etc*

CONDITIONAL		*IMPERATIVE*
PRESENT	PAST	
1 avrei	avrei avuto	
2 avresti	avresti avuto	abbi
3 avrebbe	avrebbe avuto	abbia
1 avremmo	avremmo avuto	abbiamo
2 avreste	avreste avuto	abbiate
3 avrebbero	avrebbero avuto	abbiano

SUBJUNCTIVE		
PRESENT	IMPERFECT	PLUPERFECT
1 abbia	avessi	avessi avuto
2 abbia	avessi	avessi avuto
3 abbia	avesse	avesse avuto
1 abbiamo	avessimo	avessimo avuto
2 abbiate	aveste	aveste avuto
3 abbiano	avessero	avessero avuto

PASSATO PROSSIMO	abbia avuto *etc*

INFINITIVE	*GERUND*	*PAST PARTICIPLE*
PRESENT	avendo	avuto
avere		
PAST		
aver(e) avuto		

DARE to give

	PRESENT	IMPERFECT	FUTURE
1	do	davo	darò
2	dai	davi	darai
3	dà	dava	darà
1	diamo	davamo	daremo
2	date	davate	darete
3	danno	davano	daranno

	PASSATO REMOTO	PASSATO PROSSIMO	PLUPERFECT
1	dièdi/detti	ho dato	avevo dato
2	desti	hai dato	avevi dato
3	diede/dette	ha dato	aveva dato
1	demmo	abbiamo dato	avevamo dato
2	deste	avete dato	avevate dato
3	diedero/dettero	hanno dato	avevano dato

PAST ANTERIOR	FUTURE PERFECT
ebbi dato *etc*	avrò dato *etc*

CONDITIONAL		*IMPERATIVE*
PRESENT	**PAST**	
1 darei	avrei dato	
2 daresti	avresti dato	dà/dai/da'
3 darebbe	avrebbe dato	dia
1 daremmo	avremmo dato	diamo
2 dareste	avreste dato	date
3 darebbero	avrebbero dato	diano

SUBJUNCTIVE		
PRESENT	**IMPERFECT**	**PLUPERFECT**
1 dia	dessi	avessi dato
2 dia	dessi	avessi dato
3 dia	desse	avesse dato
1 diamo	dessimo	avessimo dato
2 diate	deste	aveste dato
3 diano	dessero	avessero dato

PASSATO PROSSIMO	abbia dato *etc*

INFINITIVE	*GERUND*	*PAST PARTICIPLE*
PRESENT	dando	dato
dare		
PAST		
aver(e) dato		

DIRE to say, tell

PRESENT	IMPERFECT	FUTURE
1 dico	dicevo	dirò
2 dici	dicevi	dirai
3 dice	diceva	dirà
1 diciamo	dicevamo	diremo
2 dite	dicevate	direte
3 dicono	dicevano	diranno

PASSATO REMOTO	PASSATO PROSSIMO	PLUPERFECT
1 dissi	ho detto	avevo detto
2 dicesti	hai detto	avevi detto
3 disse	ha detto	aveva detto
1 dicemmo	abbiamo detto	avevamo detto
2 diceste	avete detto	avevate detto
3 dissero	hanno detto	avevano detto

PAST ANTERIOR		FUTURE PERFECT
ebbi detto *etc*		avrò detto *etc*

CONDITIONAL		IMPERATIVE
PRESENT	PAST	
1 direi	avrei detto	
2 diresti	avresti detto	di'
3 direbbe	avrebbe detto	dica
1 diremmo	avremmo detto	diciamo
2 direste	avreste detto	dite
3 direbbero	avrebbero detto	dicano

SUBJUNCTIVE		
PRESENT	IMPERFECT	PLUPERFECT
1 dica	dicessi	avessi detto
2 dica	dicessi	avessi detto
3 dica	dicesse	avesse detto
1 diciamo	dicessimo	avessimo detto
2 diciate	diceste	aveste detto
3 dicano	dicessero	avessero detto

PASSATO PROSSIMO	abbia detto *etc*

INFINITIVE	GERUND	PAST PARTICIPLE
PRESENT	dicendo	detto
dire		
PAST		
aver(e) detto		

DOVERE to have to, owe

PRESENT	IMPERFECT	FUTURE
1 devo/debbo	dovevo	dovrò
2 devi	dovevi	dovrai
3 deve	doveva	dovrà
1 dobbiamo	dovevamo	dovremo
2 dovete	dovevate	dovrete
3 devono/debbono	dovevano	dovranno

PASSATO REMOTO	PASSATO PROSSIMO	PLUPERFECT
1 dovei/dovetti	ho dovuto	avevo dovuto
2 dovesti	hai dovuto	avevi dovuto
3 dové/dovette	ha dovuto	aveva dovuto
1 dovemmo	abbiamo dovuto	avevamo dovuto
2 doveste	avete dovuto	avevate dovuto
3 doverono/dovettero	hanno dovuto	avevano dovuto

PAST ANTERIOR		FUTURE PERFECT
ebbi dovuto *etc*		avrò dovuto *etc*

CONDITIONAL PRESENT	PAST	IMPERATIVE
1 dovrei	avrei dovuto	
2 dovresti	avresti dovuto	
3 dovrebbe	avrebbe dovuto	
1 dovremmo	avremmo dovuto	
2 dovreste	avreste dovuto	
3 dovrebbero	avrebbero dovuto	

SUBJUNCTIVE PRESENT	IMPERFECT	PLUPERFECT
1 deva/debba	dovessi	avessi dovuto
2 deva/debba	dovessi	avessi dovuto
3 deva/debba	dovesse	avesse dovuto
1 dobbiamo	dovessimo	avessimo dovuto
2 dobbiate	doveste	aveste dovuto
3 devano/debbano	dovessero	avessero dovuto

PASSATO PROSSIMO	abbia dovuto *etc*

INFINITIVE PRESENT	GERUND	PAST PARTICIPLE
dovere	dovendo	dovuto
PAST		
aver(e) dovuto		

NOTE: in compound tenses 'dovere' takes the same auxiliary as the following verb, eg: I had to go = sono dovuto/a andare; I had to read = ho dovuto leggere

ESSERE to be

PRESENT	IMPERFECT	FUTURE
1 sono	ero	sarò
2 sei	eri	sarai
3 è	era	sarà
1 siamo	eravamo	saremo
2 siete	eravate	sarete
3 sono	erano	saranno

PASSATO REMOTO	PASSATO PROSSIMO	PLUPERFECT
1 fui	sono stato/a	ero stato/a
2 fosti	sei stato/a	eri stato/a
3 fu	è stato/a	era stato/a
1 fummo	siamo stati/e	eravamo stati/e
2 foste	siete stati/e	eravate stati/e
3 furono	sono stati/e	erano stati/e

PAST ANTERIOR	FUTURE PERFECT
fui stato/a *etc*	sarò stato/a *etc*

CONDITIONAL		*IMPERATIVE*
PRESENT	**PAST**	
1 sarei	sarei stato/a	
2 saresti	saresti stato/a	sii
3 sarebbe	sarebbe stato/a	sia
1 saremmo	saremmo stati/e	siamo
2 sareste	sareste stati/e	siate
3 sarebbero	sarebbero stati/e	siano

SUBJUNCTIVE		
PRESENT	**IMPERFECT**	**PLUPERFECT**
1 sia	fossi	fossi stato/a
2 sia	fossi	fossi stato/a
3 sia	fosse	fosse stato/a
1 siamo	fossimo	fossimo stati/e
2 siate	foste	foste stati/e
3 siano	fossero	fossero stati/e

PASSATO PROSSIMO	sia stato/a *etc*

INFINITIVE	*GERUND*	*PAST PARTICIPLE*
PRESENT	essendo	stato/a/i/e
essere		
PAST		
esser(e) stato/a/i/e		

ESSERE AMATO to be loved

	PRESENT	IMPERFECT	FUTURE
1	sono amato/a	ero amato/a	sarò amato/a
2	sei amato/a	eri amato/a	sarai amato/a
3	è amato/a	era amato/a	sarà amato/a
1	siamo amati/e	eravamo amati/e	saremo amati/e
2	siete amati/e	eravate amati/e	sarete amati/e
3	sono amati/e	erano amati/e	saranno amati/e

	PASSATO REMOTO	PASSATO PROSSIMO	PLUPERFECT
1	fui amato/a	sono stato/a amato/a	ero stato/a amato/a
2	fosti amato/a	sei stato/a amato/a	eri stato/a amato/a
3	fu amato/a	è stato/a amato/a	era stato/a amato/a
1	fummo amati/e	siamo stati/e amati/e	eravamo stati/e amati/e
2	foste amati/e	siete stati/e amati/e	eravate stati/e amati/e
3	furono amati/e	sono stati/e amati/e	erano stati/e amati/e

PAST ANTERIOR	FUTURE PERFECT
fui stato/a amato/a *etc*	sarò stato/a amato/a *etc*

CONDITIONAL		*IMPERATIVE*
PRESENT	**PAST**	
1 sarei amato/a	sarei stato/a amato/a	
2 saresti amato/a	saresti stato/a amato/a	
3 sarebbe amato/a	sarebbe stato/a amato/a	
1 saremmo amati/e	saremmo stati/e amati/e	
2 sareste amati/e	sareste stati/e amati/e	
3 sarebbero amati/e	sarebbero stati/e amati/e	

SUBJUNCTIVE		
PRESENT	**IMPERFECT**	**PLUPERFECT**
1 sia amato/a	fossi amato/a	fossi stato/a amato/a
2 sia amato/a	fossi amato/a	fossi stato/a amato/a
3 sia amato/a	fosse amato/a	fosse stato/a amato/a
1 siamo amati/e	fossimo amati/e	fossimo stati/e amati/e
2 siate amati/e	foste amati/e	foste stati/e amati/e
3 siano amati/e	fossero amati/e	fossero stati/e amati/e

PASSATO PROSSIMO	sia stato/a amato/a *etc*

INFINITIVE	*GERUND*	*PAST PARTICIPLE*
PRESENT	essendo amato/a/i/e	essendo stato/a/i/e
esser(e) amato/a/i/e		amato/a/i/e
PAST		
esser(e) stato/a/i/e amato/a/i/e		

FARE to do, make

	PRESENT	IMPERFECT	FUTURE
1	faccio	facevo	farò
2	fai	facevi	farai
3	fa	faceva	farà
1	facciamo	facevamo	faremo
2	fate	facevate	farete
3	fanno	facevano	faranno

	PASSATO REMOTO	PASSATO PROSSIMO	PLUPERFECT
1	feci	ho fatto	avevo fatto
2	facesti	hai fatto	avevi fatto
3	fece	ha fatto	aveva fatto
1	facemmo	abbiamo fatto	avevamo fatto
2	faceste	avete fatto	avevate fatto
3	fecero	hanno fatto	avevano fatto

PAST ANTERIOR	FUTURE PERFECT
ebbi fatto *etc*	avrò fatto *etc*

CONDITIONAL		*IMPERATIVE*
PRESENT	**PAST**	
1 farei	avrei fatto	
2 faresti	avresti fatto	fa/fai/fa'
3 farebbe	avrebbe fatto	faccia
1 faremmo	avremmo fatto	facciamo
2 fareste	avreste fatto	fate
3 farebbero	avrebbero fatto	facciano

SUBJUNCTIVE		
PRESENT	**IMPERFECT**	**PLUPERFECT**
1 faccia	facessi	avessi fatto
2 faccia	facessi	avessi fatto
3 faccia	facesse	avesse fatto
1 facciamo	facessimo	avessimo fatto
2 facciate	faceste	aveste fatto
3 facciano	facessero	avessero fatto

PASSATO PROSSIMO	abbia fatto *etc*

INFINITIVE	*GERUND*	*PAST PARTICIPLE*
PRESENT	facendo	fatto
fare		
PAST		
aver(e) fatto		

FINIRE to finish, end

	PRESENT	IMPERFECT	FUTURE
1	finisco	finivo	finirò
2	finisci	finivi	finirai
3	finisce	finiva	finirà
1	finiamo	finivamo	finiremo
2	finite	finivate	finirete
3	finiscono	finivano	finiranno

	PASSATO REMOTO	PASSATO PROSSIMO	PLUPERFECT
1	finii	ho finito	avevo finito
2	finisti	hai finito	avevi finito
3	finì	ha finito	aveva finito
1	finimmo	abbiamo finito	avevamo finito
2	finiste	avete finito	avevate finito
3	finirono	hanno finito	avevano finito

PAST ANTERIOR	FUTURE PERFECT
ebbi finito *etc*	avrò finito *etc*

CONDITIONAL		*IMPERATIVE*
PRESENT	**PAST**	
1 finirei	avrei finito	
2 finiresti	avresti finito	finisci
3 finirebbe	avrebbe finito	finisca
1 finiremmo	avremmo finito	finiamo
2 finireste	avreste finito	finite
3 finirebbero	avrebbero finito	finiscano

SUBJUNCTIVE		
PRESENT	**IMPERFECT**	**PLUPERFECT**
1 finisca	finissi	avessi finito
2 finisca	finissi	avessi finito
3 finisca	finisse	avesse finito
1 finiamo	finissimo	avessimo finito
2 finiate	finiste	aveste finito
3 finiscano	finissero	avessero finito

PASSATO PROSSIMO	abbia finito *etc*

INFINITIVE	*GERUND*	*PAST PARTICIPLE*
PRESENT	finendo	finito
finire		
PAST		
aver(e) finito		

LAVARSI to have a wash

	PRESENT	IMPERFECT	FUTURE
1	mi lavo	mi lavavo	mi laverò
2	ti lavi	ti lavavi	ti laverai
3	si lava	si lavava	si laverà
1	ci laviamo	ci lavavamo	ci laveremo
2	vi lavate	vi lavavate	vi laverete
3	si lavano	si lavavano	si laveranno

	PASSATO REMOTO	PASSATO PROSSIMO	PLUPERFECT
1	mi lavai	mi sono lavato/a	mi ero lavato/a
2	ti lavasti	ti sei lavato/a	ti eri lavato/a
3	si lavò	si è lavato/a	si era lavato/a
1	ci lavammo	ci siamo lavati/e	ci eravamo lavati/e
2	vi lavaste	vi siete lavati/e	vi eravate lavati/e
3	si lavarono	si sono lavati/e	si erano lavati/e

PAST ANTERIOR		FUTURE PERFECT
mi fui lavato/a *etc*		mi sarò lavato/a *etc*

CONDITIONAL		*IMPERATIVE*
PRESENT	PAST	
1 mi laverei	mi sarei lavato/a	
2 ti laveresti	ti saresti lavato/a	lavati
3 si laverebbe	si sarebbe lavato/a	si lavi
1 ci laveremmo	ci saremmo lavati/e	laviamoci
2 vi lavereste	vi sareste lavati/e	lavatevi
3 si laverebbero	si sarebbero lavati/e	si lavino

SUBJUNCTIVE		
PRESENT	IMPERFECT	PLUPERFECT
1 mi lavi	mi lavassi	mi fossi lavato/a
2 ti lavi	ti lavassi	ti fossi lavato/a
3 si lavi	si lavasse	si fosse lavato/a
1 ci laviamo	ci lavassimo	ci fossimo lavati/e
2 vi laviate	vi lavaste	vi foste lavati/e
3 si lavino	si lavassero	si fossero lavati/e

PASSATO PROSSIMO	mi sia lavato/a *etc*

INFINITIVE	*GERUND*	*PAST PARTICIPLE*
PRESENT	lavandomi *etc*	lavato/a/i/e
lavarsi		
PAST		
essersi lavato/a/i/e		

POTERE to be able to

	PRESENT	IMPERFECT	FUTURE
1	posso	potevo	potrò
2	puoi	potevi	potrai
3	può	poteva	potrà
1	possiamo	potevamo	potremo
2	potete	potevate	potrete
3	possono	potevano	potranno

	PASSATO REMOTO	PASSATO PROSSIMO	PLUPERFECT
1	potei/potetti	ho potuto	avevo potuto
2	potesti	hai potuto	avevi potuto
3	poté/potette	ha potuto	aveva potuto
1	potemmo	abbiamo potuto	avevamo potuto
2	poteste	avete potuto	avevate potuto
3	poterono/potettero	hanno potuto	avevano potuto

PAST ANTERIOR	FUTURE PERFECT
ebbi potuto *etc*	avrò potuto *etc*

CONDITIONAL		*IMPERATIVE*
PRESENT	PAST	
1 potrei	avrei potuto	
2 potresti	avresti potuto	
3 potrebbe	avrebbe potuto	
1 potremmo	avremmo potuto	
2 potreste	avreste potuto	
3 potrebbero	avrebbero potuto	

SUBJUNCTIVE		
PRESENT	IMPERFECT	PLUPERFECT
1 possa	potessi	avessi potuto
2 possa	potessi	avessi potuto
3 possa	potesse	avesse potuto
1 possiamo	potessimo	avessimo potuto
2 possiate	poteste	aveste potuto
3 possano	potessero	avessero potuto

PASSATO PROSSIMO	abbia potuto *etc*

INFINITIVE	*GERUND*	*PAST PARTICIPLE*
PRESENT	potendo	potuto
potere		
PAST		
aver(e) potuto		

NOTE: In compound tenses 'potere' takes the same auxiliary as the following verb, eg: I was able to come = sono potuto/a venire; I was able to eat = ho potuto mangiare

SAPERE to know, know how to

PRESENT	IMPERFECT	FUTURE
1 so	sapevo	saprò
2 sai	sapevi	saprai
3 sa	sapeva	saprà
1 sappiamo	sapevamo	sapremo
2 sapete	sapevate	saprete
3 sanno	sapevano	sapranno

PASSATO REMOTO	PASSATO PROSSIMO	PLUPERFECT
1 seppi	ho saputo	avevo saputo
2 sapesti	hai saputo	avevi saputo
3 seppe	ha saputo	aveva saputo
1 sapemmo	abbiamo saputo	avevamo saputo
2 sapeste	avete saputo	avevate saputo
3 seppero	hanno saputo	avevano saputo

PAST ANTERIOR		FUTURE PERFECT
ebbi saputo *etc*		avrò saputo *etc*

CONDITIONAL PRESENT	PAST	*IMPERATIVE*
1 saprei	avrei saputo	
2 sapresti	avresti saputo	sappi
3 saprebbe	avrebbe saputo	sappia
1 sapremmo	avremmo saputo	sappiamo
2 sapreste	avreste saputo	sappiate
3 saprebbero	avrebbero saputo	sappiano

SUBJUNCTIVE PRESENT	IMPERFECT	PLUPERFECT
1 sappia	sapessi	avessi saputo
2 sappia	sapessi	avessi saputo
3 sappia	sapesse	avesse saputo
1 sappiamo	sapessimo	avessimo saputo
2 sappiate	sapeste	aveste saputo
3 sappiano	sapessero	avessero saputo

PASSATO PROSSIMO	abbia saputo *etc*

INFINITIVE PRESENT	*GERUND*	*PAST PARTICIPLE*
sapere	sapendo	saputo
PAST		
aver(e) saputo		

SERVIRE to serve

	PRESENT	IMPERFECT	FUTURE
1	servo	servivo	servirò
2	servi	servivi	servirai
3	serve	serviva	servirà
1	serviamo	servivamo	serviremo
2	servite	servivate	servirete
3	servono	servivano	serviranno

	PASSATO REMOTO	PASSATO PROSSIMO	PLUPERFECT
1	servii	ho servito	avevo servito
2	servisti	hai servito	avevi servito
3	servì	ha servito	aveva servito
1	servimmo	abbiamo servito	avevamo servito
2	serviste	avete servito	avevate servito
3	servirono	hanno servito	avevano servito

PAST ANTERIOR	FUTURE PERFECT
ebbi servito *etc*	avrò servito *etc*

CONDITIONAL		*IMPERATIVE*
PRESENT	**PAST**	
1 servirei	avrei servito	
2 serviresti	avresti servito	servi
3 servirebbe	avrebbe servito	serva
1 serviremmo	avremmo servito	serviamo
2 servireste	avreste servito	servite
3 servirebbero	avrebbero servito	servano

SUBJUNCTIVE		
PRESENT	**IMPERFECT**	**PLUPERFECT**
1 serva	servissi	avessi servito
2 serva	servissi	avessi servito
3 serva	servisse	avesse servito
1 serviamo	servissimo	avessimo servito
2 serviate	serviste	aveste servito
3 servano	servissero	avessero servito

PASSATO PROSSIMO	abbia servito *etc*

INFINITIVE	*GERUND*	*PAST PARTICIPLE*
PRESENT	servendo	servito
servire		
PAST		
aver(e) servito		

STARE to be

	PRESENT	IMPERFECT	FUTURE
1	sto	stavo	starò
2	stai	stavi	starai
3	sta	stava	starà
1	stiamo	stavamo	staremo
2	state	stavate	starete
3	stanno	stavano	staranno

	PASSATO REMOTO	PASSATO PROSSIMO	PLUPERFECT
1	stetti	sono stato/a	ero stato/a
2	stesti	sei stato/a	eri stato/a
3	stette	è stato/a	era stato/a
1	stemmo	siamo stati/e	eravamo stati/e
2	steste	siete stati/e	eravate stati/e
3	stettero	sono stati/e	erano stati/e

PAST ANTERIOR	FUTURE PERFECT
fui stato/a *etc*	sarò stato/a *etc*

	CONDITIONAL PRESENT	PAST	*IMPERATIVE*
1	starei	sarei stato/a	
2	staresti	saresti stato/a	sta/stai/sta`
3	starebbe	sarebbe stato/a	stia
1	staremmo	saremmo stati/e	stiamo
2	stareste	sareste stati/e	state
3	starebbero	sarebbero stati/e	stiano

	SUBJUNCTIVE PRESENT	IMPERFECT	PLUPERFECT
1	stia	stessi	fossi stato/a
2	stia	stessi	fossi stato/a
3	stia	stesse	fosse stato/a
1	stiamo	stessimo	fossimo stati/e
2	stiate	steste	foste stati/e
3	stiano	stessero	fossero stati/e

PASSATO PROSSIMO	
sia stato/a *etc*	

INFINITIVE PRESENT	*GERUND*	*PAST PARTICIPLE*
stare	stando	stato/a/i/e
PAST		
esser(e) stato/a/i/e		

TEMERE to fear, be afraid of

	PRESENT	IMPERFECT	FUTURE
1	temo	temevo	temerò
2	temi	temevi	temerai
3	teme	temeva	temerà
1	temiamo	temevamo	temeremo
2	temete	temevate	temerete
3	temono	temevano	temeranno

	PASSATO REMOTO	PASSATO PROSSIMO	PLUPERFECT
1	temei/temetti	ho temuto	avevo temuto
2	temesti	hai temuto	avevi temuto
3	temé/temette	ha temuto	aveva temuto
1	tememmo	abbiamo temuto	avevamo temuto
2	temeste	avete temuto	avevate temuto
3	temerono/temettero	hanno temuto	avevano temuto

PAST ANTERIOR	FUTURE PERFECT
ebbi temuto *etc*	avrò temuto *etc*

	CONDITIONAL PRESENT	PAST	*IMPERATIVE*
1	temerei	avrei temuto	
2	temeresti	avresti temuto	temi
3	temerebbe	avrebbe temuto	tema
1	temeremmo	avremmo temuto	temiamo
2	temereste	avreste temuto	temete
3	temerebbero	avrebbero temuto	temano

	SUBJUNCTIVE PRESENT	IMPERFECT	PLUPERFECT
1	tema	temessi	avessi temuto
2	tema	temessi	avessi temuto
3	tema	temesse	avesse temuto
1	temiamo	temessimo	avessimo temuto
2	temiate	temeste	aveste temuto
3	temano	temessero	avessero temuto

PASSATO PROSSIMO	abbia temuto *etc*

INFINITIVE PRESENT	*GERUND*	*PAST PARTICIPLE*
temere	temendo	temuto
PAST		
aver(e) temuto		

TENERE to hold

PRESENT	IMPERFECT	FUTURE
1 tengo	tenevo	terrò
2 tieni	tenevi	terrai
3 tiene	teneva	terrà
1 teniamo	tenevamo	terremo
2 tenete	tenevate	terrete
3 tengono	tenevano	terranno

PASSATO REMOTO	PASSATO PROSSIMO	PLUPERFECT
1 tenni	ho tenuto	avevo tenuto
2 tenesti	hai tenuto	avevi tenuto
3 tenne	ha tenuto	aveva tenuto
1 tenemmo	abbiamo tenuto	avevamo tenuto
2 teneste	avete tenuto	avevate tenuto
3 tennero	hanno tenuto	avevano tenuto

PAST ANTERIOR	FUTURE PERFECT
ebbi tenuto *etc*	avrò tenuto *etc*

CONDITIONAL		*IMPERATIVE*
PRESENT	**PAST**	
1 terrei	avrei tenuto	
2 terresti	avresti tenuto	tieni
3 terrebbe	avrebbe tenuto	tenga
1 terremmo	avremmo tenuto	teniamo
2 terreste	avreste tenuto	tenete
3 terrebbero	avrebbero tenuto	tengano

SUBJUNCTIVE		
PRESENT	**IMPERFECT**	**PLUPERFECT**
1 tenga	tenessi	avessi tenuto
2 tenga	tenessi	avessi tenuto
3 tenga	tenesse	avesse tenuto
1 teniamo	tenessimo	avessimo tenuto
2 teniate	teneste	aveste tenuto
3 tengano	tenessero	avessero tenuto

PASSATO PROSSIMO	abbia tenuto *etc*

INFINITIVE	*GERUND*	*PAST PARTICIPLE*
PRESENT	tenendo	tenuto
tenere		
PAST		
aver(e) tenuto		

VENIRE to come

PRESENT	IMPERFECT	FUTURE
1 vengo	venivo	verrò
2 vieni	venivi	verrai
3 viene	veniva	verrà
1 veniamo	venivamo	verremo
2 venite	venivate	verrete
3 vengono	venivano	verranno

PASSATO REMOTO	PASSATO PROSSIMO	PLUPERFECT
1 venni	sono venuto/a	ero venuto/a
2 venisti	sei venuto/a	eri venuto/a
3 venne	è venuto/a	era venuto/a
1 venimmo	siamo venuti/e	eravamo venuti/e
2 veniste	siete venuti/e	eravate venuti/e
3 vennero	sono venuti/e	erano venuti/e

PAST ANTERIOR		FUTURE PERFECT
fui venuto/a *etc*		sarò venuto/a *etc*

CONDITIONAL PRESENT	PAST	*IMPERATIVE*
1 verrei	sarei venuto/a	
2 verresti	saresti venuto/a	
3 verrebbe	sarebbe venuto/a	vieni
1 verremmo	saremmo venuti/e	venga
2 verreste	sareste venuti/e	veniamo
3 verrebbero	sarebbero venuti/e	venite
		vengano

SUBJUNCTIVE PRESENT	IMPERFECT	PLUPERFECT
1 venga	venissi	fossi venuto/a
2 venga	venissi	fossi venuto/a
3 venga	venisse	fosse venuto/a
1 veniamo	venissimo	fossimo venuti/e
2 veniate	veniste	foste venuti/e
3 vengano	venissero	fossero venuti/e

PASSATO PROSSIMO	sia venuto/a *etc*

INFINITIVE PRESENT	GERUND	*PAST PARTICIPLE*
venire	venendo	venuto/a/i/e
PAST		
esser(e) venuto/a/i/e		

VOLERE to want

	PRESENT	IMPERFECT	FUTURE
1	voglio	volevo	vorrò
2	vuoi	volevi	vorrai
3	vuole	voleva	vorrà
1	vogliamo	volevamo	vorremo
2	volete	volevate	vorrete
3	vogliono	volevano	vorranno

	PASSATO REMOTO	PASSATO PROSSIMO	PLUPERFECT
1	volli	ho voluto	avevo voluto
2	volesti	hai voluto	avevi voluto
3	volle	ha voluto	aveva voluto
1	volemmo	abbiamo voluto	avevamo voluto
2	voleste	avete voluto	avevate voluto
3	vollero	hanno voluto	avevano voluto

PAST ANTERIOR	FUTURE PERFECT
ebbi voluto *etc*	avrò voluto *etc*

CONDITIONAL		IMPERATIVE
PRESENT	**PAST**	
1 vorrei	avrei voluto	
2 vorresti	avresti voluto	
3 vorrebbe	avrebbe voluto	
1 vorremmo	avremmo voluto	
2 vorreste	avreste voluto	
3 vorrebbero	avrebbero voluto	

SUBJUNCTIVE		
PRESENT	**IMPERFECT**	**PLUPERFECT**
1 voglia	volessi	avessi voluto
2 voglia	volessi	avessi voluto
3 voglia	volesse	avesse voluto
1 vogliamo	volessimo	avessimo voluto
2 vogliate	voleste	aveste voluto
3 vogliano	volessero	avessero voluto

PASSATO PROSSIMO	abbia voluto *etc*

INFINITIVE	GERUND	PAST PARTICIPLE
PRESENT	volendo	voluto
volere		
PAST		
aver(e) voluto		

NOTE: in compound tenses as an auxiliary 'volere' takes the same auxiliary as the following verb, eg: I wanted to eat = ho voluto mangiare; I wanted to go = sono voluto/a andare

P. VERB CONSTRUCTIONS

In Italian there are two main types of verb construction. Verbs can be followed:

1. by another verb in the infinitive
2. by an object (a noun or a pronoun)

1. Verbs followed by an infinitive

There are four main constructions where a verb is followed by an infinitive:

a) verb + infinitive (without any linking preposition)
b) verb + **di** + infinitive
c) verb + **a** + infinitive
d) verb + **da** + infinitive

For examples of these four types of construction, see pp 149-52.

* asterisked verbs also admit other constructions.

a) *Verbs followed by an infinitive without preposition*

adorare	to adore (doing)
amare	to love (doing, to do)
*bastare	to be enough (to do)
bisogna (*impers*)	to need (to do)
convenire	to be worthwhile (doing)
*desiderare	to want (to do), to wish (to do)
dovere	to have to (do)
fare	to make (do)
giovare	to be useful (to do)
importare	to be important (to do)
*lasciare	to let (do), to allow (to do)
occorrere	to be necessary (to do)
osare	to dare (to do)
*piacere	to like (doing, to do)
potere	to be able to (do)
preferire	to prefer (doing, to do)
sapere	to know how (to do)
*sembrare	to seem (to do)
sentire	to feel (doing), to hear (doing)
solere	to be used to (doing)
toccare	to be one's turn (to do)
udire	to hear (doing)
vedere	to see (doing)
volere	to want (to do)

mi piacerebbe vederti	**tocca a te telefonargli**
I'd like to see you	it's your turn to phone him/them

b) *Verbs followed by* **di** + *infinitive*

accettare di	to agree (to do)
accorgersi di	to notice (that), to realize (that)
accusare di	to accuse of (doing)
ammettere di	to admit to (doing)
*aspettare di	to wait (to do)
aspettarsi di	to expect (to do)
assicurare di	to assure (that)
augurare di	to wish (to do)
*badare di	to be careful (to do), to make sure (of doing)
capitare di	to happen (to do)
cercare di	to try (to do)
cessare di	to cease (doing), to stop (doing)
chiedere di	to ask (to do)
comandare di	to order (to do)
concedere di	to allow (to do)
consigliare di	to advise (to do)
contentarsi di	to content oneself with (doing)
credere di	to believe (that)
decidere di	to decide (to do)
dichiarare di	to declare (that)
dimenticare di	to forget (to do)
dimostrare di	to prove (that), to show (that)
dire di	to say (to do), to tell (to do)
*dispiacere di	to be sorry (to do)
dubitare di	to doubt (that)
escludere di	to exclude the possibility of (doing)
evitare di	to avoid (doing)
far conto di	to suppose (that)
figurarsi di	to imagine (that)
fingere di	to pretend (that)
finire di	to finish (doing)
giurare di	to swear (to do)
godere di	to enjoy (doing)
*guardare di	to take care (to do)
illudersi di	to delude oneself (that)
immaginarsi di	to think (that), to imagine (that)
impedire di	to prevent (from doing)
incaricare di	to ask (to do)
interessarsi di	to be interested in (doing)
mancare di	to fail (to do)
meravigliarsi di	to be amazed at (doing)

meritare di	to deserve (to do)
offrire di	to offer (to do)
ordinare di	to order (to do)
***parere di**	to seem (to do)
parlare di	to talk (of doing)
pensare di	to think (of doing)
pentirsi di	to repent (of having done)
permettere di	to allow (to do)
***piacere di**	to like (to do, doing)
pregare di	to pray (to do), to ask (to do)
preoccuparsi di	to worry about (doing), to trouble (to do)
pretendere di	to claim (to do)
proibire di	to forbid (to do)
promettere di	to promise (to do)
raccomandare di	to beg (to do), to exhort (to do)
rallegrarsi di	to be pleased (that)
ricordarsi di	to remember (to do/doing)
rifiutare di	to refuse (to do)
rincrescere di	to be sorry (to do)
scegliere di	to choose (to do)
scrivere di	to write (to do)
scusare di	to excuse (for doing)
***sembrare di**	to seem (that)
***sentire di**	to feel (that)
sforzarsi di	to try hard (to do)
smettere di	to stop (doing)
sognare di	to dream (of doing)
sopportare di	to put up (with doing)
sospettare di	to suspect (of doing)
sperare di	to hope (to do)
supplicare di	to beg (to do)
temere di	to fear (doing)
tentare di	to attempt (to do)
vantarsi di	to boast (that)
vergognarsi di	to be ashamed (of doing)
vietare di	to forbid (to do)

c) *Verbs followed by* **a** + *infinitive*

abituare a	to accustom (to doing)
abituarsi a	to get used (to doing)
accennare a	to make as if (to do), to look as if
accondiscendere a	to agree (to do)
acconsentire a	to consent (to do)
affrettarsi a	to rush (to do)
aiutare a	to help (to do)

andare a	to go (to do)
arrischiarsi a	to dare (to do)
arrivare a	to manage (to do)
*aspettare a	to wait (to do)
aspirare a	to have aspirations (to do)
* badare a	to mind (that)
cominciare a	to begin (to do)
concorrere a	to contribute (to doing)
condannare a	to condemn (to do)
consentire a	to consent (to do)
continuare a	to go on (doing)
contribuire a	to contribute (to doing)
convincere a	to persuade (to do)
costringere a	to compel (to do)
destinare a	to destine (to do)
divertirsi a	to enjoy (doing)
esercitarsi a	to practise (doing)
esitare a	to hesitate (to do)
giocare a	to play (at doing)
imparare a	to learn (to do)
impegnarsi a	to undertake (to do), to be engaged in (doing)
incitare a	to incite (to do)
indurre a	to induce (to do)
insegnare a	to teach (to do)
insistere a	to insist (on doing)
invitare a	to invite (to do)
mandare a	to send (to do)
mettersi a	to start (to do, doing)
obbligare a	to force (to do)
persuadere a	to persuade (to do)
prepararsi a	to get ready (to do)
provare a	to try (to do)
provvedere a	to see to (doing)
rassegnarsi a	to resign oneself (to doing)
rinunciare a	to give up (doing)
riprendere a	to start (to do) again
riuscire a	to succeed (in doing)
sbrigarsi a	to hurry up (and do)
servire a	to be useful (for doing)
spingere a	to urge (to do)
tardare a	to be late (in doing)
tenerci a	to be keen (on doing)
tornare a	to return (to doing), to go back (to doing)
venire a	to come (to do)

d) *Verbs followed by **da** + infinitive* (this construction is less common)

astenersi da	to abstain (from doing)
avere da	to have to (do)
contenersi da	to restrain oneself (from doing)
***diffidare da**	to warn (against doing)
dissuadere da	to dissuade (from doing)
guardarsi da	to be careful of (doing), to beware of (doing)

Note also the following constructions:

mi ha dato da mangiare
he/she gave me something to eat

fare da mangiare **lui paga da bere**
to make something to eat he's buying the drinks

2. Verbs followed by an object

In general, verbs which take a direct object in Italian also take a direct object in English, and verbs which take an indirect object in Italian (ie verb + preposition + object) also take an indirect object in English. There are however some exceptions:

a) Some common verbs followed by an indirect object in English but not in Italian (the English preposition is not translated):

ascoltare	to listen to
aspettare	to wait for
attendere	to wait for
cercare	to look for
chiedere	to ask for
domandare	to ask for
far pagare	to charge for
guardare	to look at
pagare	to pay for

chiediamo il conto!
let's ask for the bill!

cercava le pantofole
he/she was looking for his/her slippers

b) Some verbs which take a direct object in English, but **a** + indirect object in Italian:

assomigliare a	to resemble
avvicinarsi a	to approach
concedere a	to allow

convenire a	to suit
disubbidire a	to disobey
far piacere a	to please
giocare a	to play (*game, sport*)
perdonare a	to forgive
piacere a	to please
resistere a	to resist
rinunciare a	to give up
rispondere a	to answer
telefonare a	to phone
ubbidire a	to obey

telefoni all'editore
ring the publisher

vuoi giocare a scacchi?
do you want to play chess?

c) Verbs which take a direct object in English but **di** + indirect object in Italian:

accorgersi di	to notice
aver bisogno di	to need
diffidare/non fidarsi di	to mistrust
dubitare di	to doubt
fidarsi di	to trust
impadronirsi di	to seize
mancare di	to lack, to miss
ricordarsi di	to remember
servirsi di	to use

fidatevi della nostra esperienza
trust our experience

lui manca assolutamente di tatto
he is absolutely lacking in tact

mi sono sempre ricordato del tuo compleanno
I have always remembered your birthday

d) Some verbs take **di** or **a** before an object, whereas their English equivalent uses a different preposition:

i) verb + **di** + object:

incolpare di	to charge with
innamorarsi di	to fall in love with
meravigliarsi di	to wonder at
parlare di	to speak about
ridere di	to laugh at

riempire di	to fill with
ringraziare di	to thank for
trattarsi di	to be about, to be a question of
vivere di	to live on

non si tratta di soldi
it's not a question of money

devo ringraziarvi della vostra cortesia
I must thank you for your kindness

vivevano di espedienti
they lived by their wits

riempirono i bicchieri di vino frizzante
they filled their glasses with sparkling wine

ii) verb + **a** + object:

credere a	to believe
interessarsi a	to be interested in
pensare a	to think of/about

pensava solo alla sua moto
he/she only thought of his/her motorbike

credo a quello che dici
I believe what you say

e) Other constructions use different prepositions in English and Italian:

dipendere da	to depend on
parlare con	to speak to
entrare in	to enter

3. Verbs followed by one direct object and one indirect object

a) This is a very wide category of verbs. In general they are constructed in the same way as their English equivalents:

spiegare qualcosa a qualcuno
to explain something to somebody

ho venduto un pezzo di giardino ai miei vicini
I've sold a piece of my garden to my neighbours

Note: in this type of construction the preposition 'to' is often omitted in English, but **a** cannot be omitted in Italian, and particular care must be taken when object pronouns are used (see pp 71-2)

b) With verbs expressing the idea of 'taking away', **a** is translated by 'from' (**qn** = **qualcuno**, 'sb' = somebody, **qc** = **qualcosa** and 'sth' = something):

chiedere qc a qn	to ask sb for sth
domandare qc a qn	to ask sb for sth
levare qc a qn	to take sth away from sb
nascondere qc a qn	to hide sth from sb
portare via qc a qn	to take sth away from somebody
prendere qc a qn	to take sth from sb
rubare qc a qn	to steal sth from sb
togliere qc a qn	to take sth away from sb

Alberto ci nascose la sua malattia
Alberto concealed his illness from us

non portargli via la palla
don't take his ball away from him

hanno rubato la valigia a mia madre
they have stolen my mother's suitcase

4. Verb + indirect object + *di* + infinitive

Some verbs which take a direct object in English are followed by **a** + object + **di** + infinitive in Italian.

chiedere a qn di fare qc	to ask sb to do sth
comandare a qn di fare qc	to order sb to do sth
consigliare a qn di fare qc	to advise sb to do sth
dire a qn di fare qc	to tell sb to do sth
domandare a qn di fare qc	to ask sb to do sth
ordinare a qn di fare qc	to order sb to do sth
permettere a qn di fare qc	to allow sb to do sth
proibire a qn di fare qc	to forbid sb to do sth
promettere a qn di fare qc	to promise sb to do sth
proporre a qn di fare qc	to offer to do sth for sb, to suggest to sb to do sth

chiedi alla segretaria di aiutarti
ask the secretary to help you

ordinò alla pattuglia di andare in perlustrazione
he ordered the patrol to go on reconnaissance

hanno promesso ai loro genitori di rientrare presto
they promised their parents that they would get home early

8. PREPOSITIONS

a) The following are prepositions which combine with the definite article to produce a single word (**preposizioni articolate**):

a	to	**su**	on
di	of	(**per**	by, through)
da	from, by	(**con**	with)
in	in		

Note: the combined forms with **per** will be found primarily in older written texts and are relatively rare in the modern spoken or written language; this is also true for the majority of the combined forms with **con**, only **col** and **coi** being still common:

	il	lo	l'	i	gli	la	l'	le
a	al	allo	all'	ai	agli	alla	all'	alle
di	del	dello	dell'	dei	degli	della	dell'	delle
da	dal	dallo	dall'	dai	dagli	dalla	dall'	dalle
in	nel	nello	nell'	nei	negli	nella	nell'	nelle
su	sul	sullo	sull'	sui	sugli	sulla	sull'	sulle
(**per**	pel	etc)						
(**con**	col	etc)						

che cos'hai detto alla mamma?
what did you say to Mum?

la macchina dello zio
my uncle's car

è tornato ieri dagli Stati Uniti
he returned yesterday from the United States

ha cercato un libro sullo scaffale
he/she looked for a book on the shelf

c'è un po' d'insalata nel frigo
there's a little salad in the fridge

mangio l'insalata col/con il limone
I eat salad with lemon juice

b) The following prepositions usually take the preposition **di** before a pronoun:

contro*	against
dentro*	inside
dietro*	behind

dopo	after
fra/tra	among, between
presso*	near, c/o, almost
senza	without
sopra*	above, upon
sotto	under
su	on
verso	towards

contro di te against you	**dopo di lei** after her/you
dentro di me inside me	**su di esso** on it
senza di lui without him	**verso di loro** towards them

The asterisked prepositions may also take **a** before a noun although
in most cases this is less common:

dietro la casa/dietro alla casa
behind the house

il vescovado si trova dietro al duomo
the bishop's residence is behind the cathedral

dietro di lei c'è un posto libero
there's an empty seat behind you/her

presso al liceo c'è un'edicola
there's a newspaper kiosk near the school

a Roma abitava presso una famiglia
he/she used to live with a family in Rome

mia zia abita presso di noi
my aunt lives with us

Note: with **fra/tra** the preposition is sometimes omitted:

loro s'intendono molto bene fra (di) loro
they get along very well together

and also **fra me e te c'è stato un malinteso**
there's been a misunderstanding between us

c) Prepositional phrases:

i)
accanto a beside	**incontro a** towards
addosso a beside, right next to	**innanzi a** before
circa a regarding	**insieme a** along with, together
davanti a in front of, before	**intorno a** around
dinanzi a in front of, before	**quanto a** as for, as regards
dirimpetto a opposite	**riguardo a** regarding
fino/sino a up to, until	**rispetto a** regarding
	vicino a near

mi sono seduta accanto a lui
I sat down next to him

c'è un lavasecco dirimpetto all'appartamento
there's a dry cleaner's opposite the flat

quanto a mio marito, può venire più tardi
as for my husband, he can come later on

abitano vicino a una centrale nucleare
they live near a nuclear power station

Note: **dirimpetto** also functions as an invariable adjective in which case it must follow the noun:

i miei suoceri abitano nel palazzo dirimpetto
my parents-in-law live in the block of flats opposite

ii) | | |
|---|---|
| **in capo a** | at the head of, at the top of |
| **in cima a** | at the top of, at the summit of |
| **in faccia a** | opposite, facing |
| **in fondo a** | at the bottom of |
| **di fronte a** | in front of, opposite, facing |
| **in mezzo a** | in the middle of |
| **in testa a** | at the head of |

in cima alla montagna   **in fondo alla strada**
at the top of the mountain   at the bottom of the street

di fronte al duomo   **in mezzo alla pianura**
in front of the cathedral   in the middle of the plain

d) Prepositional phrases with **di**:

a causa di	because of, on account of
fuori di	out, outside
invece di	instead of
per mezzo di	by means of
prima di	before

il treno è bloccato a causa della neve
the train can't get through because of the snow

purtroppo Mario è fuori di casa
unfortunately Mario is not at home

ci è arrivato prima di me
he got there before I did

Note, however, the set expression:

fuori città
out of town

e) Prepositional phrases with **da**:

fin (sin) da	(as) from, ever since
lontano da	far from
lungi da	far from

fin da bambina mi è sempre piaciuto
I've liked it ever since I was a child

ha dovuto posteggiare lontano dal teatro
he/she had to park far away from the theatre

f) Other prepositions:

attraverso across	**mediante** by means of, through
durante during	**nonostante** in spite of
eccetto except	**salvo** except
fuorché except	**secondo** according to
malgrado in spite of	**tranne** except

attraverso il Tevere	**durante la tempesta**
across the Tiber	during the storm
malgrado i miei dubbi	**secondo me, è un errore**
in spite of my doubts	in my opinion, it's a mistake

g) Prepositional verbs:

These are not as common in Italian as they are in English. But some typical examples are:

buttare giù	**mettere su**
to jot down	to set up

buttai giù due righe
I jotted down a few lines

hanno messo su casa insieme
they've set up house together

Note: for verbs requiring a preposition before a dependent infinitive, see pp 190-6.

---

a (ad)

Note: **ad** may be substituted for **a** when the following word begins with a vowel (particularly the same vowel)

(dative function)   **l'ho regalato ad Angelo**
                      I made Angelo a present of it

(place at/to which)	**sono rimasto/andato a casa** I stayed at/went home
	hanno una casa al mare they have a house at the seaside
	andiamo al mare let's go to the seaside
	sono ancora a letto I'm still in bed
	è andato a letto tardi he went to bed late
	domani andremo a scuola we'll be going to school tomorrow
Note:	a is always used with the names of towns or cities
	abita a Pistoia he/she lives in Pistoia
	ogni tanto vado a Roma I go to Rome every so often
(direction)	**a nord/a sud di Firenze** north/south of Florence
	mi voltai a destra/a sinistra I turned right/left
(distance)	**a venti chilometri da Barga** twenty kilometres from Barga
	a pochi metri dall'incrocio a few metres from the crossroads
(time)	**a che ora parte? - alle undici** what time are you leaving? - at eleven
	a Natale/Pasqua at Christmas/Easter
	una volta al giorno/alla settimana once a day/a week
	a domani! see you tomorrow!
(with adverbial phrases of time or quantity)	**a poco a poco** little by little
	a due a due two by two

	un poco alla volta a little at a time
	a centinaia/migliaia by the hundreds/thousands
	a volte sometimes
	a vita for life
(with certain adjectives)	**pronto a partire** ready to leave
	disposto ad aiutare willing to help
(after ordinals, **solo, unico**)	**il primo ad andarsene** the first to go away
	il solo a pagare the only one to pay
(manner)	**risotto alla milanese** risotto Milanese style
	carne alla griglia grilled meat
	spaghetti al pomodoro spaghetti with tomato sauce
	tè al limone tea with lemon
	a bocca aperta with one's mouth open
	ad alta/a bassa voce in a loud/low voice
	a mia insaputa unbeknown to me
	imparare a memoria to learn by heart
	chiudere a chiave to lock
	dipinto a mano hand-painted
(means of transport or method of operation)	**andare a piedi** to go on foot

una barca a remi/a vela
a rowing/sailing boat

un motore a reazione
a jet engine

(invocation)	**al fuoco!** fire!
	al ladro! stop thief!
(games)	**giocare a tennis** to play tennis
	giocare a scacchi to play chess
(after many verbs)	see pp 195-6

con

(association)	**vieni con me** come with me
(manner)	**ha parlato con una voce rauca** he/she spoke in a hoarse voice
	accettare con piacere to accept with pleasure
	procedere con calma to proceed calmly
(means)	**con un coltello** with a knife
	fare di sì/di no con la testa to nod/shake one's head
(idiom)	**non possiamo andare con questa pioggia** we can't go in this rain
	e con questo? so what?
	con mia grande sorpresa to my great surprise
	con mio gran dolore to my great sorrow

da

Note:	**di** may be elided before a vowel but **da** never is
(origin)	**Leonardo da Vinci** *literally* Leonardo from Vinci
But:	**sono di Bari** I'm from Bari

(motion from)	**da Pisa a Lucca** from Pisa to Lucca
	arrivo da Genova alle tre I'm arriving from Genoa at three
(manner)	**agire da pazzo** to act like a madman
	si è comportato da bambino he acted like a child
	vestire da pirata to dress up like a pirate
	da vicino/da lontano close up/from a distance
	andare da solo to go by oneself
	fare tutto da sé to do everything oneself
(to or at someone's house or business premises)	**vieni da me stasera** come to my house tonight
	siamo andati dai Rossi we went to the Rossi's
	andare dal dentista/medico to go to the dentist's/doctor's
	andare dal parrucchiere to go to the hairdresser's
(purpose)	**una macchina da scrivere** a typewriter
	un tavolo da stiro an ironing board **uno spazzolino da denti** a toothbrush **un costume da bagno** a swimming costume **la stanza da bagno** the bathroom **la camera da letto** the bedroom **il vino da tavola** table wine **una casa da affittare** a house to let
	una tazza da caffè a coffee cup
But:	**una tazza di caffè** a cup of coffee
(physical description)	**la ragazza dai capelli rossi** the girl with red hair

	il signore dall'aspetto elegante the elegant-looking gentleman
(monetary value)	**un biglietto da cinquantamila lire** a fifty thousand lire note
	un francobollo da 650 lire a 650 lire stamp
(length of time)	**abito a Glasgow da quattro anni** I've been living in Glasgow for four years
	lavoravo da sei mesi I had been working for six months
Note:	for tenses with **da** see pp 129-30
(cause)	**morire dal freddo** to die of cold
	tremare dalla paura to shake with fright
(before an infinitive)	**pazzo da legare** mad as a hatter **niente da dire** nothing to say **molto da fare** a lot to do **c'è un freddo da morire** it's freezing cold **un problema da risolvere** a problem to solve **il prezzo da pagare** the price to be paid
(idiom)	**è un uomo da poco** he's a worthless sort of man
	da giovane mi piaceva ballare when I was young I liked dancing
	da piccolo/da vecchio as a child/as an old man
	da una parte... dall'altra on the one hand ... on the other hand
	da parte mia on my part, on my behalf
(passive)	**la cena è stata offerta da mio cognato** the dinner was hosted by my brother-in-law

di

Note:	if followed by a vowel **di** becomes **d'**
(genitive)	**il canarino del nonno** grandfather's canary

	il presidente della repubblica the president of the republic
	il sistema dei trasporti the transport system
(specification)	**l'isola d'Elba** the Island of Elba **la città di Modena** the city of Modena
(in partitives)	**ho comprato delle albicocche** I bought some apricots
	ci vuole un po' di sale it needs a little salt
(origin)	**sono di Ascoli Piceno** I'm from Ascoli Piceno
	un vino della Toscana a wine from Tuscany
(motion from)	**è già partito di casa** he has already left home
(number or quantity)	**un chilo di patate** a kilo of potatoes
	un paio di scarpe a pair of shoes
	venti litri di benzina twenty litres of petrol
	un milione d'abitanti one million inhabitants
(time)	**di giorno/di notte** by day/by night
	di mattina/di sera in the morning/in the evening
	sono le sei di mattina it's six in the morning
	d'estate/d'inverno in the summer/in the winter
(age)	**un bambino di due anni** a two-year-old child
	una donna d'una certa età a middle-aged woman
(composition or contents)	**una camicetta di seta** a silk blouse **un vestito di lana** a woollen dress

una catena d'oro a gold chain
una bottiglia di vino a bottle of wine
un bicchiere d'acqua a glass of water

(manner)

di malavoglia
unwillingly, reluctantly

di nascosto
furtively

essere di malumore/di buonumore
to be ill-humoured/good-humoured

è andata via di corsa
she ran off

(after certain adjectives)

è contento di rimanere a casa
he is happy to stay at home

sono degni di rispetto
they are worthy of respect

quell'armadio è pieno di roba
that cupboard is full of stuff

era vestita di bianco/nero
she was dressed in white/black

(after many verbs)

morire di fame to die of hunger
piangere di gioia to weep for joy

Note: see pp 190-1 for verbs which take **di** before a dependent infinitive

(with comparatives before nouns, pronouns and numerals)

hai viaggiato più di Stefano
you have travelled more than Stefano

hai letto più di me
you've read more than me

meno di cinque persone
fewer than five people

(after superlatives)

il calciatore più famoso del mondo
the most famous footballer in the world

(idiom)

cosa c'è di nuovo? what's new?
niente di grave nothing serious
lo conosco di vista I know him by sight
dire di sì/di no) to say yes/no

dare del tu/del lei a qualcuno
to use the **tu/lei** form with someone

in

(place in which or to which)	**essere/andare in cucina** to be in/go to the kitchen
	essere/andare in ufficio to be in/go to the office
	abitare/andare in centro to live in/go to the town centre
	avere una casa in campagna to have a house in the country

Note: use **in** with regions, countries, large islands and continents:

in Liguria ci sono molte stazioni balneari
in Liguria there are many holiday resorts

Treviso è nel Veneto
Treviso is in the Veneto

siamo in Francia/negli Stati Uniti per affari
we are in France/in the States on business

in Sardegna d'estate ci sono molti turisti
in Sardinia in the summer there are a lot of tourists

la sua famiglia è emigrata in Australia
his/her/your family emigrated to Australia

(expressions of time)	**in primavera/in autunno** in the spring/in the autumn
	gli Italiani vanno in ferie in agosto Italians go on holiday in August
	nel 1945 è finita la guerra the war ended in 1945
	viviamo nel Novecento we are living in the twentieth century
	il treno è arrivato in orario/in ritardo the train arrived on time/late

(modes of transport)	**viaggiare in aereo/in treno/in pullman** to travel by air/by train/by bus
	andare in bicicletta to cycle

(manner)	**vivere in miseria** to live in poverty **studiare in pace** to study in peace **ascoltare in silenzio** to listen in silence

è partito in fretta he left in a hurry
fatto in casa home-made

(idiom) **credere in Dio**
to believe in God

eravamo in sette
there were seven of us

parlare in italiano/inglese
to speak in Italian/in English

è molto bravo in lingue ma non in matematica
he's very good at languages but not at maths

questa rivista è stata offerta in omaggio
this magazine was a free gift

stare in piedi to stand
balzai in piedi I leapt to my feet

per

(intended for) **questo pacco è per te**
this parcel is for you

(duration) **siamo qui per alcuni giorni**
we are here for a few days

sono rimasta a Venezia per una settimana
I stayed in Venice for a week

(destination) **sono partiti per Torino**
they left for Turin

(purpose) **la crema per scarpe**
shoe polish

sono venuto per ringraziarti
I've come to thank you

(means) **chiamare per telefono**
to call by phone

mandare una lettera per via aerea
to send a letter by airmail

viaggiare per terra/per mare
to travel by land/by sea

(place) **vagava per le strade**
he/she was wandering through the streets

l'ho incontrato per strada
I met him in the street

l'hanno trovato disteso **per terra**
they found him lying on the ground

buttalo per terra
throw it on the ground

correre su/giù per la strada/le scale
to run up/down the street/the stairs

per di qua! this way!
per di là that way!

(with **stare**) **sta per annegare** he's/she's going to drown
stavano per pagare they were about to pay

(idiom) **per favore/per piacere/per cortesia**
please
per modo di dire so to speak
per fortuna fortunately
per caso by chance

---

su

(place on which) **sul tavolo c'era una bottiglia**
on the table there was a bottle

il gatto era sdraiato sul tappeto
the cat was stretched out on the carpet

(onto, literally **il cane è saltato sul muro**
and figuratively) the dog jumped onto the wall

la casa dà sul mare
the house looks out onto the sea

(on, about) **fece una conferenza sulla Cee**
he/she gave a lecture about the EEC

(about, approx.) **è un uomo sulla cinquantina**
he's a man of about fifty

la valigia sarà sui venti chili
the case must be about twenty kilos

(out of) **nove volte su dieci**
nine times out of ten

(idiom) **non mi hai mai preso sul serio**
you have never taken me seriously

l'ho letto sul giornale
I read it in the newspaper

---

9. CONJUNCTIONS

Conjunctions are invariable parts of speech which link words, phrases or clauses. They can consist of one word or several words (conjunctive phrases).

Conjunctive words:

e	o	ma
and	or	but

Conjunctive phrases:

con tutto ciò	anche se	di modo che
in spite of it all	even though	so that

Conjunctions fall into two categories:

A. coordinating
B. subordinating

A. COORDINATING CONJUNCTIONS

1. Definition

Coordinating conjunctions link two similar words or groups of words. The following are the principal coordinating conjunctions (or adverbs used as conjunctions):

e	anche	pure
and	also	also
né	neanche	nemmeno
nor	not even	not even
o	oppure	altrimenti
or	or, otherwise	otherwise, or else
ma	tuttavia	però
but	yet, however, nevertheless	but, yet, however nevertheless

infatti as a matter of fact, actually	**cioè** that is, namely	**ossia** that is, or rather
dunque so, therefore	**perciò** so, therefore	**pertanto** so, therefore
quindi so, therefore	**ebbene** well (then)	**allora** then

aveva fame e sete
he/she was hungry and thirsty

prendere o lasciare
take it or leave it

se avrò tempo andrò a piedi, altrimenti in bicicletta
if I have time I'll walk, otherwise I'll go on my bike

aveva poco tempo per cucinare, perciò comprò un forno a micro-onde
he/she had little time to cook, so he/she bought a microwave

Note:

i) when the conjunction **e** is placed in front of another vowel - **e** in particular - it is often changed to **ed**:

è intelligente ed equilibrata
she's intelligent and well-balanced

il pane e(d) il vino
bread and wine

ii) when **ma** is used to connect two clauses, a comma or a semicolon is always placed before it. When it joins two words or phrases in the same clause, no comma is added:

uscì di casa, ma non andò a lavorare
he/she left home but did not go to work

uno scolaro intelligente ma pigro
an intelligent but lazy schoolboy

2. Correlative conjunctions

e ... e and ... and	**ora ... ora** sometimes ... sometimes
o ... o either ... or	**né ... né** neither ... nor
non solo ... ma anche not only ... but also	**tanto ... quanto** as ... as

non c'era nessuno né alla fermata dell'autobus né al posteggio dei
taxi
there was no-one either at the bus stop or at the taxi rank

non solo si mise a piovere ma cominciò anche a grandinare
not only did it begin to rain, but it also began to hail

ora ride, ora piange
sometimes he/she smiles, sometimes he/she cries

B. SUBORDINATING CONJUNCTIONS

1. Definition

These introduce a clause that cannot stand on its own as a full
sentence but is dependent on another one, usually a main clause.

a patto che/a condizione che on condition that	**mentre** while, whereas
al punto che so much that	**nel senso che** in the sense that
che that	**(non) appena** as soon as
come how, like, as soon as	**ogni volta che** every time that
come se as if	**perché** why, because
comunque however	**per quanto** although, even though
dal momento che since	**poiché** as, since
dato che given that	**prima che** before
dopo che after	**purché** provided that
dove where	**qualora** in case
finché until	**quando** when

fin tanto che as long as	**quantunque** although
giacché as, since	**se** if
in modo che so that, in such a way	**senza che** without

siccome
as, since, because

era tanto stanco che non riuscì a chiudere occhio
he was so tired that he did not manage to sleep at all

siccome una lettera non sarebbe arrivata in tempo mandarono un fax
since a letter would not have arrived in time they sent a fax

voglio vedere dei miglioramenti prima che finisca il trimestre
I want to see some improvement before the term is over

la salutò come se la conoscesse
he/she greeted her as if he/she knew her

2. Conjunctions which are almost always used with the subjunctive

perché so that	**affinché** so that	**che** so that
benché (al)though	**sebbene** (al)though	**per quanto** although
nonostante che even though in spite of	**purché** provided that	

parla ad alta voce affinché tutti sentano
he/she speaks loudly so that everyone can hear

sebbene sia passato tanto tempo continua a parlarne
although so much time has gone by he/she goes on talking about it

3. Correlative conjunctions

più ... che more ... than	**meno ... che** less ... than
più ... di quanto more ... than	**meglio/peggio ... che** better/worse ... than

la lavastoviglie consuma più elettricità di quanto non immaginassi
the dishwasher uses up more electricity than I imagined

C. USE OF CONJUNCTIONS HAVING MORE THAN ONE MEANING

1. PERCHÉ

a) When **perché** means 'because' or 'why', it is followed by the indicative:

> **perché non hai preso l'ombrello? perché faceva bel tempo quando sono uscito**
> why didn't you take your umbrella? because when I went out the weather was fine

> **ieri non si alzò perché non si sentiva bene**
> yesterday he/she did not get up because he/she was not feeling well

b) When **perché** means 'so that', it is followed by the subjunctive:

> **ti telefono perché tu sappia quello che sta succedendo**
> I'm ringing so that you know what's happening

2. SE

a) When **se** introduces an *if* clause, it is followed either by the subjunctive or by the indicative (see p 143):

> **se mangiasse di meno non ingrasserebbe tanto**
> if he/she ate less, he/she wouldn't put on so much weight

> **perderai il treno se non corri**
> you'll miss the train, if you don't run

b) When **se** expresses doubt, it is followed by the conditional or by the infinitive:

> **mi chiedo se accetterebbe questa proposta**
> I wonder if he/she would accept this proposal

> **non sapeva se ridere o piangere**
> he/she didn't know whether to laugh or cry

3. *CHE*

a) When **che** means 'that', it could be followed by the subjunctive or the indicative (see also p 131):

> **disse che lo aveva visto**
> he/she said that he/she had seen him

> **penso che tu abbia ragione**
> I think that you're right

> **non è prudente che vi mettiate in viaggio ora**
> it is not wise that you begin your journey now

> **spero che vi divertiate**
> I hope that you enjoy yourselves

b) When **che** means 'so that', it is followed by the subjunctive:

> **spiegai chiaramente la regola, che tutti potessero capire**
> I explained the rule clearly, so that everyone could understand

Note: some conjunctions such as **dove, come, quando, perché** etc could also be adverbs:

quando parti?	**telefonami quando arrivi**
when are you leaving?	ring me up when you arrive
(*adverb*)	(*conjunction*)

10. NUMBERS AND QUANTITY

A. CARDINAL NUMBERS

0	zero	27	ventisette
1	uno	28	ventotto
2	due	29	ventinove
3	tre	30	trenta
4	quattro	40	quaranta
5	cinque	50	cinquanta
6	sei	60	sessanta
7	sette	70	settanta
8	otto	80	ottanta
9	nove	90	novanta
10	dieci	100	cento
11	undici	101	centouno
12	dodici	200	duecento
13	tredici	300	trecento
14	quattordici	400	quattrocento
15	quindici	500	cinquecento
16	sedici	600	seicento
17	diciassette	700	settecento
18	diciotto	800	ottocento
19	diciannove	900	novecento
20	venti	1000	mille
21	ventuno	1992	millenovecento-novantadue
22	ventidue		
23	ventitré	2,000	duemila
24	ventiquattro	5,000	cinquemila
25	venticinque	10,000	diecimila
26	ventisei	100,000	centomila

un milione, due milioni
one million, two million

un miliardo, due miliardi
one billion, two billion

Note:

a) 'One' used on its own has two forms: **uno** (*masc*) and **una** (*fem*):

> **ne voglio uno/una**
> I want one

'One' used in front of a noun behaves like an indefinite article and takes endings (**un, uno, una, un'**):

> **un libro**
> one/a book
>
> **uno studente**
> one/a student
>
> **una sterlina**
> one/a pound
>
> **un'isola**
> one/an island

b) The tens from **venti** to **novanta** lose their final vowel in front of **uno** and **otto**:

> **venti, ventuno, ventotto**
> twenty, twenty-one, twenty-eight

c) **Cento** and **mille** are never preceded by one as in English. When preceded by other numbers, **cento** remains invariable:

> **trecento**
> three hundred

whilst **mille** changes to **mila**:

> **duemila**
> two thousand

d) Compounds with **uno** lose their final **-o** in front of a noun:

> **ventun ragazzi**
> twenty-one boys

e) Compounds ending with **-tré** always have an acute accent:

> **ventitré**
> twenty-three

f) **Milione** and **miliardo** have plural forms and are always followed by **di** when used with a noun:

> **tre milioni di persone**
> three million people

g) Points not commas are used to separate thousands (**diecimila** is written 10.000) and commas not points are used for decimals:

uno virgola sei *or* **1,6**
one point six *or* 1.6

h) All numbers, single or compound, are written as one word but **e** (and) is often used to join hundreds to units or tens:

cento e uno	**duecento e tre**
a hundred and one	two hundred and three

and to join thousands to units/tens/hundreds:

mille e due	a thousand and two
tremila e sessanta	three thousand and sixty
diecimila e cinquecento	ten thousand five hundred

i) Numbers from 200 to 900 are used to express centuries as follows:

il Duecento	the 13th century *or* the years between 1200 and 1299
il Trecento	the 14th century
il Quattrocento	the 15th century
il Cinquecento	the 16th century
il Seicento	the 17th century
il Settecento	the 18th century
l'Ottocento	the 19th century
il Novecento	the 20th century

It is also possible to use Roman numerals:

nel XIX (diciannovesimo) secolo
in the 19th century

j) Approximate numbers

una decina	about ten
una dozzina	about twelve
una quindicina	about fifteen
una ventina	about twenty
una trentina ecc.	about thirty etc
un centinaio	about a hundred
due centinaia ecc.	about two hundred etc
un migliaio	about a thousand
due migliaia	about two thousand

Note: **di** is used when approximate numbers are followed by a noun:

una decina di giorni	**un centinaio di persone**
about ten days	about a hundred people

Note: **vado a fare due/quattro passi**
I'm going for a short walk

dille tutto in due parole
tell her everything in a few words

B. ORDINAL NUMBERS

		abbreviations
1st	**primo, prima, primi, prime**	$1°,1^a,1^i,1^e$
2nd	**secondo, ecc.**	$2°,2^a,2^i,2^e$
3rd	**terzo**	$3°$ ecc.
4th	**quarto**	$4°$
5th	**quinto**	$5°$
6th	**sesto**	$6°$
7th	**settimo**	$7°$
8th	**ottavo**	$8°$
9th	**nono**	$9°$
10th	**decimo**	$10°$
11th	**undicesimo**	$11°$
12th	**dodicesimo**	$12°$
13th	**tredicesimo**	$13°$
14th	**quattordicesimo**	$14°$
15th	**quindicesimo**	$15°$
16th	**sedicesimo**	$16°$
17th	**diciassettesimo**	$17°$
18th	**diciottesimo**	$18°$
19th	**diciannovesimo**	$19°$
20th	**ventesimo**	$20°$
21st	**ventunesimo**	$21°$
22nd	**ventiduesimo**	$22°$
23rd	**ventitreesimo**	$23°$
28th	**ventottesimo**	$28°$
29th	**ventinovesimo**	$29°$
30th	**trentesimo**	$30°$
100th	**centesimo**	$100°$
101st	**centounesimo**	$101°$
200th	**duecentesimo**	$200°$
1,000th	**millesimo**	$1.000°$
10,000th	**decimillesimo**	$10.000°$

Note:

a) Ordinal numbers after **decimo** are formed by adding **-esimo** to the cardinal number which drops its final vowel except in the case of **tre** and numbers ending in **-tré**.

) Ordinal numbers belong to the class of adjectives ending in **-o/a/i/e**. These agree with the noun in gender and number and usually precede it except with names of popes and kings:

il quarto giorno
the fourth day

la quinta classe
the fifth class

i primi uomini
the first men

le prime file
the first rows

papa Paolo Sesto
Pope Paul VI

re Carlo Ottavo
King Charles VIII

) Other special ordinal numbers are:

ennesimo/a/i/e
umpteenth, nth

ultimo/a/i/e
last

C. MATHEMATICAL EXPRESSIONS

1. Vulgar fractions

Vulgar fractions are expressed as in English: cardinal number followed by ordinal number:

due quinti
two fifths

tre quarti
three quarters

un quinto
a fifth

un terzo
a third

mezzo
a half

Note: the article is omitted in Italian with **mezzo**:

quattro e mezzo
four and a half

2. Decimals

The English decimal point is conveyed by a comma in Italian (see also pp 218-19):

tre virgola cinque (3,5)
three point five (3.5)

quattro virgola cinquantasei (4,56)
four point five six (4.56)

3. Percentages

Percentages are expressed as in English:

due per cento (2%)
two per cent (2%)

Note: Italian uses the definite article with percentages:

c'è stato un incremento del 2%
there has been a 2% increase

4. Arithmetic

addition	**dieci più sei**	$10 + 6$
subtraction	**otto meno tre**	$8-3$
multiplication	**sette per due** *or* **sette volte due**	7×2
division	**quattro diviso due**	$4 \div 2$
the square	**due al quadrato**	2^2
the square root	**la radice quadrata di quattro**	$\sqrt{4}$

D. MEASUREMENTS AND PRICES

1. Measurements

a) *Dimensions and weight*

Mario è alto un metro e settanta e pesa settanta chili
Mario is one metre seventy tall and weighs seventy kilos

la classe è lunga 12 metri/è 12 metri di lunghezza
the classroom is 12 metres long

la classe è larga 8 metri/è 8 metri di larghezza
the classroom is 8 metres wide

il libro è spesso 5 centimetri/è 5 cm. di spessore
the book is 5 cms thick

la mia camera misura quattro metri per cinque
my bedroom is four metres by five

b) *Distance*

quanto dista il centro? - circa tre chilometri
how far is the centre? - it's about three kilometres

ci troviamo a cinque chilometri dal mare
we are five kilometres from the sea

è lontana la stazione ferroviaria?
is the railway station far from here?

2. Prices

qual è il prezzo di una camera singola?
what is the price of a single room?

quanto costa/viene il vino alla bottiglia?
how much is a bottle of wine?

costa/viene 2.000 lire alla bottiglia
it's 2,000 lire a bottle

quanto costano/vengono le mele al chilo?
how much is a kilo of apples?

le mele sono a 2.000 lire al chilo
apples are 2,000 lire a kilo

quanto fa/quant'è in tutto?
how much is it altogether?

sono 3.500 (tremila e cinquecento) lire in tutto
that comes to 3,500 lire altogether

Note: in informal spoken language the endings **-cento** and **-mila** can be dropped:

due(mila) e quattro =	**duemilaquattrocento lire**
	two thousand four hundred lire
tre e cinquanta =	**trecentocinquanta lire**
	three hundred and fifty lire

E. EXPRESSIONS OF QUANTITY

Quantity may be expressed by an adverb, adjective or pronoun of quantity (eg. **molto, troppo** 'a lot, too much') or by a noun which names the actual quantity involved (eg. a bottle, a dozen).

1. Adverbs, adjectives and pronouns of quantity

parecchio/parecchia/parecchi/parecchie
quite a lot, several

quanto/a/i/e
how much, many

molto/a/i/e	**un mucchio (di)**
much, many, a lot (of)	much, many, a lot (of)

poco/poca/pochi/poche
little, few

un po' (di)
some, a little

troppo/a/i/e
too much, too many

troppo poco/poca/pochi/poche
too little, too few

tanto/a/i/e
so much, so many

tanto/a/i/e/... quanto/a/i/e...
as much/many ... as ...

meno
less, fewer

più
more

abbastanza
enough

la maggior parte (di)
most, the majority (of)

non ho molto tempo
I haven't got much time

ho parecchio lavoro
I have got quite a lot of work

vorrei un po' di zucchero
I'd like some sugar

pochi sono venuti
few came

hanno tanti problemi
they have a lot of problems

quante valigie ti porti?
how many cases are you taking?

abbiamo più esperienza
we have more experience

oggi ci sono meno treni
today there are fewer trains

avete abbastanza soldi?
have you got enough money?

la maggior parte della gente
most people

2. Nouns expressing quantity + *di* + noun

una scatola di
a tin/box of

una bottiglia di
a bottle of

un vasetto di
a jar of

un pacchetto di
a packet of

un boccone di
a mouthful of (food)

un cucchiaio di
a spoonful of

un sorso di
a mouthful of (drink)

un pezzo di
a piece of

un chilo di
a kilo of

un litro di
a litre of

una libbra di
a pound of

un paio di
a pair of, a couple of

una porzione di
a portion of

una fetta di
a slice of

una tazza di
a cup of

un bicchiere di
a glass of

vorrei una scatola di pomodori e un litro d'olio
I would like a tin of tomatoes and a litre of oil

ci vogliono un chilo e mezzo di farina e un paio d'uova
you need a kilo and a half of flour and a couple of eggs

3. Expressions of quantity used without a noun

When an expression of quantity is used without a noun, **di** is replaced by **ne** which goes in front of the verb (see pp 76-7):

abbiamo visitato molti musei; ne abbiamo visitati molti a Firenze
we visited a lot of museums; we visited a lot (of them) in Florence

11. EXPRESSIONS OF TIME

A. THE TIME

che ora è, che ore sono?
what time is it?

The word **ora/ore** is only used in questions. The reply is:

sono + le + number

as in the following:

a) *Full hours*

sono le due
it is 2 o'clock

sono le undici
it is 11 o'clock

But: **è l'una**
it is 1 o'clock

è mezzogiorno/mezzanotte
it is midday/midnight

b) *Half-hours*

sono le cinque e mezzo/mezza
it's half past five

è l'una e mezzo/mezza
it's half past one

But: **è la mezza**
it's half past twelve

c) *Quarter-hours*

sono le nove e un quarto
it's quarter past nine

sono le nove meno un quarto
sono le otto e tre quarti
it's quarter to nine

) *Minutes*

> **sono le sei e venti**
> it's twenty past six
>
> **sono le due meno cinque**
> it's five to two

Note: the word **minuti** is generally omitted.

) *Am and pm*

There is no direct equivalent for these terms. Italian may use 'in the morning, in the evening' as appropriate:

di mattina, del mattino	(in the morning)
am	
di/del pomeriggio	(in the afternoon)
pm	
di notte	(at night)
am	
di sera	(in the evening)
pm	

> **sono le sette del mattino**
> it's 7 am
>
> **sono le sei del pomeriggio**
> it's six pm
>
> **sono le due di notte**
> it's 2 am
>
> **sono le dieci di sera**
> it's 10 pm

The 24 hour clock is normally used for timetables, time signals etc:

> **il treno delle tredici e quindici**
> the 13.15 train
>
> **ore venti e trentacinque minuti**
> the time is 8.35 pm

) *At what time?, at..., at about..., from ... to ...*

> **a che ora parte l'aereo?**
> at what time does the plane leave?
>
> **parte alle otto e cinque**
> it leaves at 8.05

quanto dura il viaggio?
how long does the journey take?

dura due ore
it takes 2 hours

quando vedi la tua amica?
when will you be seeing your friend?

la vedo verso le quattro
I'll be seeing her at about 4

lavoro dalle nove alle cinque
I work from nine to five

B. DATE AND AGE

1. Names of months, days and seasons

a) *Months (i mesi)*

gennaio	January
febbraio	February
marzo	March
aprile	April
maggio	May
giugno	June
luglio	July
agosto	August
settembre	September
ottobre	October
novembre	November
dicembre	December

b) *Days of the week (i giorni della settimana)*

lunedì	Monday
martedì	Tuesday
mercoledì	Wednesday
giovedì	Thursday
venerdì	Friday
sabato	Saturday
domenica	Sunday

c) *Seasons (le stagioni)*

la primavera	spring
l'estate	summer

l'autunno	autumn
l'inverno	winter

For prepositions used with the seasons see p 208 .

Note: in Italian months and days are masculine, except **la domenica**, and do not have a capital letter. Note that **l'estate** is feminine.

2. Dates

a) Cardinal numbers (eg **due, tre**) are used for the days of the month except for the first:

    il ventun marzo   **l'otto giugno**
    the twenty-first of March the eighth of June

But: **il primo luglio**
    the first of July

The definite article is used but prepositions are generally omitted (of, on):

    sono nata il ventotto aprile 1961
    I was born on April 28th, 1961

    ti ho scritto il sei (di) ottobre
    I wrote to you on the sixth of October

b) The year is expressed by the full cardinal number (or by the last two figures of it), preceded by the definite article or by the day and the month. (Of course, in writing, the numeral and not the word is normally used):

    il millenovecentonovantadue 1992
    il novantadue   '92

    sono nato nel 1958
    I was born in 1958

c)

che giorno è oggi?	**oggi è sabato**
what day is it today?	today is Saturday
quanti ne abbiamo oggi?	**oggi ne abbiamo tre**
what is the date today?	today is the third
che giorno è oggi?	**oggi è il 3 (tre) giugno**
what is the date today?	today is June 3rd

    oggi è giovedì 5 (cinque) aprile
    today is Thursday, April 5th

3. Age

Age is usually expressed by the verb **avere** + number + **anni**:

quanti anni hai?	**ha trentadue anni**
how old are you?	he/she is 32
che età ha?	**a che età...?**
what age is he/she/are you?	at what age ...?

all'età di diciotto anni si diventa maggiorenni
at the age of eighteen, one comes of age

una donna di quarant'anni
a forty-year-old woman

un uomo sui quarant'anni/sulla quarantina
a man about forty years old

C. USEFUL EXPRESSIONS

sono le sei passate	it is past 6 o'clock
alle quattro precise/ in punto	at exactly 4 o'clock
verso le nove	about 9 o'clock
verso mezzanotte	about midnight
sono appena suonate le nove	it has just struck nine
allo scoccare delle tre	on the stroke of three
dalle 9 in poi/ a partire dalle 9	from 9 o'clock onwards
poco prima delle sette	shortly before seven
poco dopo le sette	shortly after seven
prima o poi	sooner or later
il più presto possibile	as soon as possible
il più tardi possibile	as late as possible
al più presto	at the earliest
al più tardi	at the latest
è tardi/presto	it is late/early
sei in ritardo/anticipo	you are late/early
mi alzo tardi	I get up late
è arrivato in ritardo	he arrived late
il treno ha venti minuti di ritardo	the train is twenty minutes late
il mio orologio è indietro di sei minuti	my watch is six minutes slow
il mio orologio è avanti di sei minuti	my watch is six minutes fast
oggi, ieri, domani	today, yesterday, tomorrow

l'altro ieri	the day before yesterday
dopodomani	the day after tomorrow
l'indomani	the next day
tre giorni fa	three days ago
fra tre giorni	in three days' time
questa settimana	this week
la settimana scorsa	last week
la settimana prossima	next week
oggi a otto	today week
quindici giorni	a fortnight
stamattina	this morning
ieri mattina	yesterday morning
domattina, domani mattina	tomorrow morning
oggi pomeriggio	this afternoon
ieri pomeriggio	yesterday afternoon
domani pomeriggio	tomorrow afternoon
stasera	this evening, tonight
ieri sera	yesterday evening, last night
domani sera	tomorrow night
stanotte	tonight, last night
lunedì	on Monday
di lunedì, il lunedì, al lunedì	on Mondays
ogni lunedì, tutti i lunedì	every Monday
un'oretta	about an hour
una mezz'ora	a half-hour, half an hour
una mezz'oretta	about half an hour
un quarto d'ora	a quarter of an hour
tre quarti d'ora	three quarters of an hour
passare il tempo (a fare)	to spend one's time (doing)
perdere tempo	to waste time
di tanto in tanto	from time to time
nel 1992	in 1992
negli anni Venti/Trenta	in the Twenties/Thirties
negli anni '20	in the 20s
nel Novecento	in the 20th century
nel XX (ventesimo) secolo	in the 20th century
un piano quinquennale	a five-year plan
un anno bisestile	a leap year
un anno civile	a calendar year
un anno luce	a light year

12. THE SENTENCE

A. WORD ORDER

Word order is usually broadly the same in Italian as in English, except in the following cases:

1. Adjectives

Many Italian adjectives follow the noun (see pp 50-2):

una ragazza *italiana*	**hai gli occhi *azzurri***
an *Italian* girl	you have *blue* eyes

2. Adverbs

In simple tenses, adverbs usually follow the verb (see p 67):

ci vado *spesso*	**farà buio *presto***
I *often* go there	it will *soon* be dark

3. Object pronouns

Unstressed object pronouns usually come before the verb (see pp 73-4):

***ti* aspetterò**	***gliel'*ha venduto**
I'll wait for *you*	he sold *it to him*

4. Noun phrases

Noun phrases are formed differently in Italian (see p 243):

una camicia di cotone	**il padre del mio amico**
a cotton shirt	my friend's father

5. Exclamations

The word order is not affected after **come**. **che** and **quanto** (used as an adjective) are usually followed by an adjective or noun :

come fa freddo!	**come canta male!**
it's so cold!	he/she sings so badly!

che brutto è stato quel viaggio!
what an awful journey that was!

che aria stanca aveva!
he/she looked so tired!

quante stupidaggini hai detto!
what a lot of silly things you said!

quanti fiori!
what a lot of flowers!

6. Verbs of motion

The normal word order with verbs of motion is verb first followed by the subject:

sta arrivando Giovanni
Giovanni is arriving

è venuta mia mamma
my mum has come

7. Emphasis

Italian word order is not as rigid as English. A different word order can convey a shift in emphasis, something that in English would often be achieved by a change in intonation. As a general rule, the emphasis in an Italian sentence lies on the last word:

Pietro me l'ha dato
Pietro gave it to me

me l'ha dato Pietro
Pietro gave it to me

B. NEGATIVE EXPRESSIONS

1. Principal negative words

no	no
non	not
non... più	no more/longer, not ... any more
non... mai	never, not ever
non... nulla	nothing, not anything
non... niente	nothing, not anything
non... nessuno	no one, not anybody, nobody
non... nessuno	not ... any, no
non... alcuno	not ... any, no
non... affatto	not ... at all

non... mica	not ... at all
non... per niente	not ... at all
non... neanche	not even
non... neppure	not even
non... nemmeno	not even
non... né... né	neither ... nor
non... che	only

Note: **non... che** (only) is less common than **solo, solamente, soltanto** (only):

non c'è che mio padre che mi capisce
only my father understands me

2. Position of negative expressions

a) *With simple tenses, the infinitive and the imperative*

Negative words enclose the verb: **non** comes before the verb and the other negative element comes after the verb:

non mi piace per niente
I don't like it at all

qui non c'è nessuno
there's no one here

su questo non c'è nessun dubbio
there's no doubt about this

non lo vogliono nemmeno vedere
they don't even want to see him

non è né nero né grigio
it's neither black nor grey

non è mica male
it's not bad at all/it's not half bad!

preferiamo non vedere nessuno
we prefer not to see anyone

ha giurato di non perdonargli mai
he/she swore never to pardon him

non dire niente!
don't say anything!

non mangiate più!
don't eat any more!

non lo ripetere mai!
never mention this to anyone!

b) *With compound tenses*

i)   in the case of **non... più, mai, affatto, mica, neanche, nemmeno** and **neppure**, **non** precedes the auxiliary but the second negative element may either precede or follow the past participle:

non è più tornata/non è tornata più
she never came back

non l'ho neppure visto/non l'ho visto neppure
I didn't even see him

non li abbiamo nemmeno letti/non li abbiamo letti nemmeno
we haven't even read them

ii) in the case of **non... nulla, niente, nessuno** and **per niente**, the second negative element follows the past participle:

non gli abbiamo promesso niente
we didn't promise him/them anything

non abbiamo invitato nessuno
we haven't invited anybody

c) *At the beginning of the sentence*

When **nessuno, mai, niente** etc are placed first in the sentence **non** is omitted:

nessuno lo sospetta
no one suspects it

nulla è cambiato
nothing has changed

né Caterina né Pino sono venuti
neither Caterina nor Pino has shown up

Note the plural verb in the last Italian example.

3.   Combinations of negative expressions

Negative expressions may be combined as follows:

non... mai più
non... più niente/nulla
non... mai niente
non... affatto
non... più nessuno
non... mai nessuno

non ci vedremo mai più
we shall never see each other again

non c'è più niente da fare
there's nothing left to be done

non ha mai niente da dire, lui
he never has anything to say

non è affatto vero   **non vedi mai nessuno**
it's not true at all   you never see anyone

dopo di te non posso più amare nessuno
after you I can't love anybody anymore

4. Negative expressions without a verb

a) *non*

ti piace? - non molto
do you like it? - not much

lo vedi spesso? - no, non tanto
do you see him often? - no, not really

b) *no*

Note in particular the following uses of **no**:

tu ci vai? - io no!
are you going? - no, I'm not!

a te piace? - a me no!   **vieni sì o no?**
do you like it? - no, I don't!   are you coming or not?

un giorno sì e uno no   **credo di no**
every other day   I don't think so/I think not

c) *niente affatto*

ti piace? - niente affatto!
do you like it? - no way!

d) *nemmeno*

noi non ci vogliamo andare - nemmeno io!
we don't want to go - neither do I!

non abbiamo mangiato nulla - nemmeno noi
we haven't eaten anything - neither have we

e) *mai più*

tornerai a Hull? - mai più
will you ever come back to Hull? - no, never

tornerai al lunapark? - mai più!
are you going back to the fair? - not likely!/never again!

C. DIRECT AND INDIRECT QUESTIONS

1. Direct questions

There are two main ways of forming direct questions in Italian.

a) by inflection of the voice: subject + verb
b) by inversion: (question word) + verb + subject

a) *Inflection*

The word order remains the same as in statements (subject + verb) but the intonation changes: the voice is raised at the end of the sentence. This is the most common question form in Italian:

parli italiano?   **sono arrivati stamattina?**
do you speak Italian?   did they arrive this morning?

Gabrio ha scritto alla nonna?
has Gabrio written to his grandmother?

la pasta fa ingrassare?   **ti piace?**
is pasta fattening?   (do) you like it?

b) *Inversion*

si è divertito il tuo amico?
did your friend have a good time?

splende il sole da voi?
is the sun shining where you are?

This is the normal form when a question word is used:

cosa sta mangiando Paolo?
what is Paolo eating?

Note: with the verb 'to be' the word order in Italian is slightly different from English, as the subject can be placed only at the beginning or at the end of the sentence:

Giovanni è studioso? OR è studioso Giovanni?
is Giovanni hardworking?

2. Indirect questions

a) *Word order*

Indirect questions can be introduced either by interrogative or question words (like **come, perché, che cosa** etc) or by the conjunction **se** 'whether/if'. The word order is usually the same as in direct questions, with or without inversion:

direct	**come ti chiami?** what is your name?
indirect	**dimmi come ti chiami** tell me what your name is
direct	**le piace il caffè?** do you like coffee?
indirect	**mi dica se le piace il caffè** tell me whether you like coffee

b)
Indirect questions may be introduced by **chiedere** or **domandare** (to ask). Particular attention should be paid to the sequence of tenses:

Simona mi chiede se ho freddo *(present)*
Simona asks me/is asking me if I am cold

mi chiese/mi ha chiesto se stavo bene *(imperfect)*
he/she asked me if I was well

domandò loro se avevano visto suo figlio *(pluperfect)*
he/she asked them if they had seen his/her son

**Marco ha chiesto a Delia se sarebbe andata
in biblioteca** *(past conditional)*
Marco asked Delia if she would be going to the library

Note:

i) in the last example English uses the present conditional but Italian MUST use the past conditional in an indirect question since the verb in the main clause is in the past tense. The same is true of any indirect sentence:

disse che avrebbe voluto ammazzarlo
he/she said he/she would like to kill him

ii)   the subjunctive may be used in place of the indicative in the
       subordinate clause particularly in more formal or literary Italian:

domandò loro se avessero visto suo figlio
he/she asked them if they had seen his/her son

Egle le chiese dove andasse
Egle asked her where she was going

3. Translation of English question tags

a)   Examples of question tags are: isn't it?, aren't you?, doesn't he?,
      won't they?, haven't you?, is it?, did you? etc.

b)   Italian doesn't use question tags as often as English. Some of them
      can, however, be translated in the following ways:

i)   by placing **vero, è vero, non è vero, no** at the end of the sentence:

è molto simpatica, vero?   **la pizza piace a tutti, no?**
she's very nice, isn't she?   everyone likes pizza, don't they?

ii)   by placing **è vero che** at the beginning of the sentence:

è vero che vorresti venire con noi?
you'd like to come with us, wouldn't you?

4. Answers ('yes' and 'no')

a)   **sì** means 'yes' and is also equivalent to longer positive answers such
      as: 'yes, it is', 'yes, I will', 'yes, he has' etc. It can be reinforced by
      certo or **certamente**:

mi scriverai? - sì, certo!
will you write to me? - (yes) of course I will

b)   **no** means 'no' and is also equivalent to longer negative answers such
      as: 'no, it isn't', 'no, I didn't etc:

è andato bene l'esame? - no, ho fatto un sacco di errori
did the exam go well? - no (it didn't), I made a lot of mistakes

13. TRANSLATION PROBLEMS

1. False friends

A considerable number of words which appear to be recognizable through English in fact have (or may have) a different meaning in Italian:

abusivo	unauthorized, unlawful (**ingiurioso** = abusive)
assistere	to attend (as well as 'to assist')
attuale	present, topical (**reale** = actual)
coincidenza	connection (eg train or bus)
combinazione	coincidence
disgrazia	misfortune, trouble (as well as 'disgrace')
editore	publisher (**redattore** = newspaper editor)
energetico	energy (**la crisi energetica** = the energy crisis)
energico	energetic
incidente	accident
manifestazione	demonstration, event
novella	short story (**romanzo** = novel)
palazzo	palace (but also 'block of flats')
pavimento	floor (**marciapiede** = pavement)
petrolio	oil (**benzina** = petrol)
sensibile	sensitive (**sensato** = sensible)
tempestivo	timely (**tempestoso** = stormy)
ultimamente	recently (**infine** = ultimately)
visita	examination, inspection (as well as 'visit')

2. Foreign borrowings in Italian

Some words may be immediately recognizable such as **sport**, **leader**, or **meeting**. Some may have been translated literally into Italian, for instance **pioggia acida** (acid rain) and **effetto serra** (greenhouse effect). In some cases, however, although the word seems to be a direct borrowing, the meaning has in fact shifted: **un night** (a night-club), **un toast** (a toasted sandwich), **un golf** (a cardigan or sweater). Sometimes both English and Italian will have borrowed from another language: eg **un colpo di stato** (a coup d'état).

3. Problems associated with parts of speech

The following sections correspond broadly to the earlier chapters in the book and should be studied in conjunction with them:

a) *Definite article*

The definite article may be obligatory in Italian but not in English. Do not feel obliged to retain it just because it is in the original:

la Scozia   Scotland   **l'Arabia Saudita**   Saudi Arabia

il coraggio è una buona qualità
courage is a good quality

l'estate è più calda della primavera
summer is hotter than spring

i vini italiani sono buoni
Italian wines are good

è vegetariano: non mangia la carne
he's a vegetarian: he doesn't eat meat

b) *Partitive*

This may be translated as *some* or *any* in English but it may also be omitted:

ho comprato del salame	I've bought some salami
vuoi del pane?	do you want any/some bread?
ha degli amici a Rimini	he/she has friends in Rimini

c) *Genitive*

la penna di mia zia	my aunt's pen
i mariti delle mie colleghe	my colleagues' husbands

sai l'indirizzo del padrone di mio padre?
do you know my father's boss's address?

or   do you know the address of my father's boss?

la politica estera del governo britannico
the British government's foreign policy

or   the foreign policy of the British government

d) *Nouns*

i) singulars and plurals

Italian habitually uses a singular in the following type of sentence:

si sono tolti il cappotto
they took off their coats

hanno messo la cartella sulla scrivania
they put their briefcases on the desk/on their desks

Some words are normally plural in Italian, however, and singular in English:

ha fatto dei notevoli progressi
he/she has made great progress

ho chiesto delle informazioni
I asked for information

But remember to be consistent if a pronoun is used:

le ho chieste (*le informazioni*)
I asked for it

A singular form does exist in some cases but it must be translated slightly differently:

un'informazione	a piece of information
una notizia	an item of news
un mobile	a piece of furniture

ii) gender

A masculine plural noun may mask a mixture of male and female: **i figli** may mean 'sons' but it may also mean 'children'.

A feminine plural noun may have to have some indication of gender added in English if it is not otherwise clear from the context:

le mie allieve
my female pupils

i fratelli Benetton present notable problems as there are actually three brothers and one sister in the family!

iii) suffixes

These should be translated in English by using one or even two adjectives:

una vecchietta	a little old lady
una bella casetta	a nice little house
una giornataccia	a really bad day
un chiacchierone	a chatterbox, a windbag
un librone	a big thick book

iv) noun phrases

A noun phrase consists of two nouns used in combination. English requires no connecting preposition and the order of the nouns is reversed:

un corso d'aggiornamento	a refresher course
una polizza d'assicurazione	an insurance policy
le previsioni del tempo	the weather forecast
uno sciopero della fame	a hunger strike
il codice della strada	the highway code
una patente di guida	a driving licence
una crisi di governo	a government crisis
i libri di testo	text books
il treno delle otto	the eight o'clock train

e) *Adjectives*

The translation of adjectives into English often involves changes in word order:

un vestito azzurro
a light-blue dress

un ragazzo piccolo e magro
a thin little boy

un giovane artista promettente
a promising young artist

la vita istituzionale e politica italiana
Italian political and institutional life

un ambiente comodo, piacevole, accogliente
a comfortable, pleasant and welcoming environment

Note:
i) in lists of either nouns or adjectives English adds 'and' between the last two elements whereas in Italian it is not required

ii) certain Italian adjectives may change their meaning according to whether they precede or follow the noun:

un povero studente	a poor/unfortunate student
uno studente povero	a poor student (not well off)

f) *Pronouns*

i) subject and object pronouns

The former are frequently omitted in Italian and may have to be reinstated in English:

ha lavorato sodo
he/she has worked hard/you have worked hard

è sul tavolo
it's on the table

The Italian neuter pronoun **lo** is frequently omitted in translation:

è chiuso, non lo sapevi?
it's closed, didn't you know?

ii) pleonastic pronouns

Particularly in the spoken language, a pronoun may be used even if the noun to which it corresponds is also present in the sentence. It will normally be omitted in English:

la pera l'ho già mangiata
I've already eaten the pear

tu ce l'hai, la macchina?
have you got the/a car?

iii) **ne**

The particle **ne** (some, any, some of it, some of them etc) is often not translated in English:

ne hai a casa? - sì, ne ho tre
have you got any/some at home? - yes, I've got three

iv) **si**

Care must be taken with the translation of the pronoun **si** as it has a number of uses in Italian - as a reflexive, a reflexive of reciprocity, in passive constructions, and as an impersonal pronoun (remember that **sì** meaning 'yes' always has an accent):

si va avanti?
shall we carry on?

si deve tagliarlo così
you have to cut it like this

ci si sente terribilmente soli
one feels awfully alone

si dice che ha torto
they/people say he's/she's/you're wrong

non si vedono spesso gli scoiattoli
you don't often see squirrels

v) **se**

It is important not to confuse **se** meaning 'if' with the pronoun:

se si vedono spesso, litigano
if they see each other often, they quarrel

se lo dice ogni tanto
he/she repeats it to himself/herself every so often

vi) possessives

These are used far more often in English than in Italian and must frequently be added in translation, particularly with parts of the body and items of clothing:

dammi la mano
give me your hand

ha infilato i pantaloni
he/she put on his/her trousers

il vestito era nuovo fiammante
his suit was brand new

una madre coi figli
a mother with her children

vii) relative pronouns

These cannot be omitted in Italian (as they frequently are in English):

il disco che ho comprato
the record (that/which) I bought

l'uomo con cui parlavo
the man (whom/that) I was speaking to

g) *Verbs*

It is vital to recognize the tenses and persons of verbs. Irregular verbs have traditionally been the cause of most problems but even regular ones can occasionally be 'misread': eg distinguish between **finirono** (they finished) and **finiranno** (they will finish), **andremo** (we shall go) and **andremmo** (we would go), **mi fermai** (I stopped) and **mi fermerai** (you will stop me).

A single tense form in Italian may give rise to a number of possible translations in English according to the context:

andavo al cinema }	I was going to the cinema
	I used to go/would go to the cinema

tornerà l'anno prossimo }	he will come back next year
	he is coming back next year
	he will be (coming) back next year
	he is going to come back next year

A verb such as **fare** is used in a very wide range of expressions in Italian and may need to be translated by many different English verbs, for example:

mi fece compagnia	he/she kept me company
hanno fatto una domanda	they asked a question
non ho fatto attenzione	I didn't pay attention
fa caldo	it's hot
facciamo una passeggiata	let's go for a walk
ho fatto un bagno	I had a bath

h) *Sequence of tenses*

Special care must be taken with some typically Italian tense sequences which differ from English:

i) with **da** meaning 'since':

da quanto siete sposati? (*present*)
how long have you been married for?

è da molto che non ti vedo (*present*)
I haven't seen you for ages

aspettavo da ore (*imperfect*)
I had been waiting for hours

ii) with a past conditional:

sapevo che sarebbe finita così
I knew it would end up like this

pensavo che ormai l'argomento sarebbe stato chiuso
I thought the subject would be closed by now

i) *Prepositions*

Direct equivalence cannot always be expected between Italian and English prepositions as the following examples with **da** (from, by) indicate:

l'uomo dai capelli scuri
the man with the dark hair

da che il mondo è mondo
ever since the world began

da un lato... dall'altro
on the one side ... on the other

vado dal macellaio
I'm going to the butcher's

English is particularly rich in phrasal verbs, ie verbs which, when followed by a preposition, take on a new meaning. The Italian examples below can all be translated by 'to look' plus a variety of prepositions and the list is by no means exhaustive:

abbassare gli occhi/lo sguardo	to look down
alzare gli occhi/lo sguardo	to look up
girare la testa	to look round
cercare un numero	to look up a number
andare a trovare un vecchio amico	to look up an old friend
le cose vanno meglio	things are looking up!
esaminare	to look over
non vedo l'ora di andarci	I'm looking forward to going there
chi si occuperà dei bambini?	who will look after the children?

4. Idioms

Both Italian and English are rich in idiomatic expressions. Where possible you should try to match an Italian idiom with an equivalent English one, but if this is not possible the meaning must be expressed in a non-idiomatic way. Remember that some idioms are more colloquial than others and may not be appropriate for the context:

pioveva a catinelle
it was bucketing down

sono rimasta male
I was taken aback

l'ho piantato in asso
I left him in the lurch

ha troppa carne sul fuoco
he has too many irons in the fire

tagliamo la corda!
let's get out of here!

sono fritto!
now I've had it!

sono al verde!
I'm broke!

questo è un altro paio di maniche
that's another kettle of fish

detto fatto
no sooner said than done

fumare come un turco
to smoke like a chimney

vivere come un cane
to lead a dog's life

menare il can per l'aia
to beat about the bush

pallido/bianco come un cencio
as white as a sheet

si è ridotta un cencio
she was a shadow of her former self

esser vecchio come Noè
to be as old as Methuselah/the hills

5. Proper names

Christian names should not normally be translated into English even where an English equivalent exists (an exception is made for names of popes and kings etc). With the names of Italian towns, islands etc, on the other hand, where an English version exists, it should be used:

Firenze	Florence
Genova	Genoa
Milano	Milan
Padova	Padua
Sardegna	Sardinia
Torino	Turin
Venezia	Venice

Similarly, Italian versions of foreign names should be translated:

Ginevra	Geneva
Londra	London
Mosca	Moscow
Parigi	Paris

Street names should be left in Italian:

abitano in via Santo Spirito 15
they live at 15, via Santo Spirito

INDEX